Grindleford .:ery Book

Grindleford School Parent Teacher Association

All the illustrations in this book were created by
Grindleford Primary School children.
Cover by Elfie Burn.
Rear Cover by Fergus Blowen
Above illustration by Emily Barnett

First published 2013

ISBN: 978-0-9567672-2-6

www.grindlefordprimaryschool.co.uk

For information contact
Grindleford.cookbook@gmail.com

For all the children at Grindleford Primary School

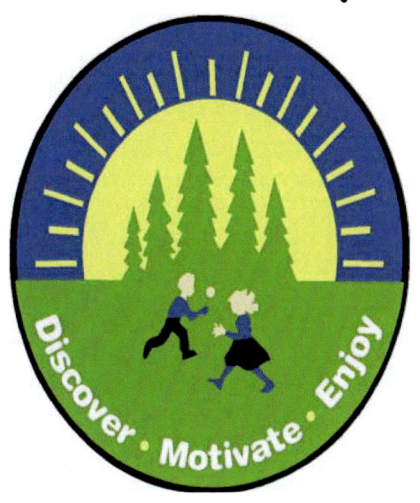

Developed by Grindleford School Parent Teacher
Association
Grindleford Primary School
Sir William Hill, Hope Valley
Derbyshire
S32 2HS
United Kingdom
www.grindlefordprimaryschool.co.uk

Contents

Forward

A school cookery book is not a new idea – it's based upon a well used formula aimed at fundraising for schools. However the Grindleford school cookery book was never going to be ordinary. Firstly the children provided many of the recipes and parents, friends and family provided many more. In this way the Cookery Book was part of the school and reflects the everyday cooking for families and children. As such it was never going to be another "Celebrity Chef" style book with extravagant recipes using impossibly expensive ingredients. (Although there are some!)

It was always intended to be the most useful cookery book in the house containing simple but tried-and-tested recipes that fit around everyday life and work. This intention has come true and a "Cook's Book" (rather than a "cookbook") has been created.

A while after we started compiling this book, a well thumbed Grindleford Primary School cookbook manuscript was found. It transpires that a Grindleford School Cookbook has been produced previously, although its year is uncertain. Past contributors, some of whom are now teachers at Grindleford primary school, have given their permission for their original

1

recipes to be used. These can be found handwritten or meticulously typed within the pages of the book.

To everyone who sponsored the book, to those who helped with the planning and provided great ideas we are indebted. Most of all however we would like to thank the children of Grindleford Primary School for their unbridled enthusiasm in providing recipes for this book.

This is *their* book and we hope *you'll* enjoy it.

Grindleford Parent Teacher Association

Grindleford Primary School in 2013

A message from the Head-teacher

Thank you for buying this book!

Not only is it a great cookery book but it's been created from the enthusiasm of Grindleford School children and the school staff. It's been helped on its way by the generosity of local business so it is a true product of the local community. All the profits go to the Parent Teacher Association. This plays a valuable role in supporting educational trips and fun activities, at the school which I am proud to be a part of.

I hope you will enjoy this book which provides not only great simple recipes, but a little insight into Grindleford School life.

Mrs Leonie Hill
Head-teacher Grindleford Primary School

Cooking with children

It can be very rewarding to spend time with children in the kitchen. It is fun (for them and for you!) and there are many learning benefits in spending time cooking with kids. Some of these are:

Encourages Creativity (so allow them to be messy!)

Helps mathematics skills by measuring, counting and following the recipe

Develops team working skills by working and sharing in the kitchen

Builds confidence

Enhances sensory skills by touching, smelling, seeing, tasting and hearing different foods

Allows you to teach them about healthy eating.

Allows you to teach them about good hygiene practices

Exposes them to a variety of foods

You get to spend time with your children – and they with you.

For younger children cooking is more exploration whereas for older children they are learning to eat cheaply and healthily:- an invaluable domestic survival skill. It's never too late to teach children how to cook – so what are you waiting for?!

Safety Tips

Prevent food poisoning by: Always washing hands before cooking. Not eating raw eggs, raw meats or uncooked foods. Waiting until the food is cooked before sampling it.

Get the children to stand at the level of the activity. Use a stool if necessary.

Use unbreakable cooking supplies (such as plastic measuring cups and stainless-steel bowls).

Use plastic knives for cutting.

Provide constant supervision. Especially watch children when they use knives, mixers, or stoves.

Explain to (and remind) children that stoves, ovens, pans, and dishes can be very hot.

Useful Information

WEIGHTS

Grams (Metric)	Ounces(oz) (Imperial)
10g	½ oz
20g	¾ oz
25g	1oz
40g	1 ½ oz
50g	2oz
60g	2 ½ oz
75g	3oz
110g	4oz
125g	5 ½ oz
150g	5oz
175g	6oz
200g	7oz
225g	8oz
250g	9oz
275g	10oz
350g	12oz
450g	16oz (1 lb)

VOLUMES (Approximate)

Millilitres (mls) (metric)	Ounces/pints (imperial)
50ml	2fl oz
75ml	3 fl oz
150mls	5fl oz (¼ pint)
275mls	10fl oz (½ pint)
550mls	20fl oz (1 pint)
1000mls (1 litre)	1 ¾ pint
1200mls (1.2l)	2 pints
1.5 litres	2 ½ pints
2.25 litres	4 pints

OVEN TEMPERATURES

Celsius	Gas Mark/Fahrenheit		
140	1	/	275F
150	2	/	300F
170	3	/	325F
180	4	/	350F
190	5	/	375F
200	6	/	400F
220	7	/	425F
230	8	/	450F
240	9	/	475F

CUP CONVERSIONS

Cups (American)	Grams (metric)	oz(imperial)
1 cup flour	150g	5oz
1 cup caster/granulated sugar	225g	8oz
1 cup brown sugar	175g	6oz
1 cup butter/margarine/lard	225g	8oz
1 cup sultanas/raisins	200g	7oz
1 cup currants	150g	5oz
1 cup ground almonds	110g	4oz
1 cup Golden Syrup	350g	12oz
1 cup uncooked rice	200g	7oz
1 cup grated cheese	110g	4oz

LIQUIDS

mls(metric)	Cups/Spoons	oz/pints (imperial)
5mls	1 teaspoon (1tsp)	$\frac{1}{6}$ fl oz
15mls	1 tablespoon (1tbsp)	$\frac{1}{2}$ fl oz
30mls	$\frac{1}{8}$ cup	1 fl oz
60mls	$\frac{1}{4}$ cup	2 fl oz
120mls	$\frac{1}{2}$ cup	4 fl oz
240mls	1 cup	8 fl oz

Thank you to our sponsors

Please see back of book for their details.

Andrew Lawton Furniture, Grindleford

Andrews of Tideswell, Coach Tours, Tideswell

The Barrel Inn, Bretton

Calver Service Station, Calver

Calver Sough Nurseries, Calver

Castlegate Farm Shop, Stoney Middleton

Cotswold Outdoor, Bakewell

Derwent Gallery, Grindleford

Educational Visual Analysis, Ilkley

Eyam Hall Buttery, Eyam

GA Shepherd, Tailor, Calver

Grindleford Private Hire, Grindleford

Hairworks, Stoney Middleton

John Mottershaw, Photography, Grindleford

The Joinery Workshop (Derbyshire) Ltd, Bakewell

Martin Heath, Electrician, Stoney Middleton

Max Codd, Building services, Grindleford

The Maynard, Grindleford

The Moon Inn, Stoney Middleton

Mount Pleasant Garage, Grindleford

Natural Earth, Grindleford

Nigel Barton, Guitar Tutor, Stoney Middleton

Outside, Hathersage

Painted Plate, Eyam

Peak Kitchen, Grindleford

Peaklander Footwear, Calver

Property Renovators, Sheffield

Stephen J Blowen, Electrician, Grindleford

The Sir William, Grindleford

Toll Bar Fish and Chips, Stoney Middleton

Regal Cleaning, Grindleford

Tideswell School of Food, Tideswell

Trees and Walls, Grindleford

The White Lion, Great Longstone

BASIL

I'm tearing the leaves

when you've only to brush them

and the kitchen's awash with the scent.

There's depth to this sauce,

tomatoes, garlic and rough red wine,

it catches my breath, tight in my throat,

sharp as our parting, salt as choked-back tears.

I'm back there then, all the way home on the train,

in my hands the pot of basil you'd grown - a gift,

the leaves, trembling tongues on their stems.

The smell was the whole train long.

Even after the journey, for hours

my hands smelled of it, my lips, my skin.

My hands smelled of it, my lips, my skin,

even after the journey, for hours.

The smell was the whole train long,

the leaves, trembling tongues on their stems,

in my hands, the pot of basil you'd grown - a gift.

I'm back there. Then all the way home on the train,

sharp as our parting, salt as choked-back tears,

it catches my breath, tight in my throat.

Tomatoes, garlic and rough red wine,

there's depth to this sauce

and the kitchen's awash with the scent.

When you've only to brush them

I'm tearing the leaves

Ann Atkinson 1947-2012. Grindleford resident who loved the village & was inspired by the Peak District landscape. Poet laureate of the Peak District in 2008 and of Derbyshire from 2009 to 2011. Reproduced with the kind permission of her two daughters, Rosie & Holly.

BASICS

BAKED POTATO

Baking potato
Oil
Salt

Wash and dry large baking potato. Prick the outside using a fork. Using a tiny amount of oil, rub the outside to coat the potato and then rub in the salt. Cook for 2 hours in oven 180°C.

POTATO WEDGES

2 potatoes per adult
Olive oil
Salt/pepper/chilli/rosemary (Optional)

Wash and chop the potatoes into small wedge shaped quarters then place in medium sized mixing bowl. Pour around 2 table spoons of olive oil in and use your hands to make sure that each potato wedge is covered. If salt/pepper etc is required add at this stage and mix in to potatoes. Place the individual wedges in rows on a baking tray, cook in oven on gas mark 6 for 45 minutes, turning half way through.

MASHED POTATO

1.5kg potatoes, peeled and quartered (Desiree, Maris Piper)
50g butter
1 cup milk
Salt and pepper to taste

Bring a large pot of water to the boil. Add potatoes and cook until tender but still firm, about 15 minutes; drain and return to large saucepan. Using a fork, potato masher or electric beater, slowly blend milk and butter into potatoes until smooth and creamy. Add salt and pepper to taste. Serves 4.
Tip: Adding Mustard or cheese works very well.

DRIED PASTA

At its simplest – follow the instructions on the packet!
Practically however, salt and oil do not need to be added to the water – as long as the pasta is separated when placed in the water – use a wooden spoon. A simple "rule of thumb" is:

One litre boiling water.
One handful dried pasta shapes per small child – 2-3 handfuls for older children/adults.
Add pasta to the boiling water and simmer for 10 minutes.
Tip: Do not cover pan or the foaming water will boil over!

Illustration by Jessica Nolan

RICE

1 cup of rice (Long Grain/Basmati/Jasmine)
2 cups of water

Place rice and water into a saucepan. Bring to boil. Cover and turn down to simmer. Leave until all water has gone.

Tip: Tilt pan from side to side to check when all water has gone. Serves 3-4.

COUSCOUS
One cup couscous
One cup water
One vegetable stock cube
25g Butter (optional)

Place Stock cube in a saucepan with water and bring to boil. Mix fully. Add couscous and turn off heat. Cover and leave for 5 minutes. Break up grains with a fork and stir in butter, mixing thoroughly. Serve immediately. Serves 3-4.

Tip: Omit the stock cube and butter; cook with just water. Stir in tomato puree at the end - a favourite with children!

SALAD DRESSING

$\frac{3}{4}$ cup oil (see note)
$\frac{1}{4}$ cup white wine vinegar
Salt and ground black pepper (optional) to taste

Place all the ingredients in a bottle (or suitable container) and shake vigorously for 30 seconds, until fully combined.
Shake again immediately prior to use. Can keep for up to 2 weeks.

Any vegetable oil is fine for this basic recipe. Experiments (such as sesame oil and balsamic vinegar) are only to be encouraged!

FROZEN PEAS

One Tablespoon peas per person.
Enough water just to cover peas in the saucepan

Place peas into a saucepan and pour in enough water just to cover them. Bring to boil stirring (to ensure all areas are boiling). Take off heat and serve.
Note. Cooking and boiling or using too much water, reduces the vitamins in the peas.

PIZZA DOUGH

3 cups strong bread flour (plain)
1 sachet (about 1 teaspoon) dried yeast
1/5cup olive oil
1cup cold water
Teaspoon sugar
Pinch of salt

Mix all the dry ingredients together thoroughly in a large bowl. Add water and oil and mix to form dough. If it's too dry it'll break apart, so add small amounts of extra water. If it's too wet it'll stick to your hands (and to the bowl) so add a small amount more flour. The aim is to have dough that is soft and does not stick to hands. Knead for 5 minutes and leave for 2 hours to rise. Knead again for 5 minutes then leave for further hour. Spread onto pizza tray.
Tip: If time is short knead for as long as possible then just spread out dough onto pizza tray and cook with toppings of your choice.

Why I Like Grindleford Primary School.......
"Because we are making chocolates today!"
Grace Marshall (Year 1)

NEVER FAIL BREAD

(You need to allow about 3 hours from putting the ingredients in the bowl, to getting it out of the oven.)

400g strong white flour, plus more for dusting and shaping
1 tsp dry instant yeast.
1 tsp fine salt
300ml warm water,
Vegetable oil for kneading

Mix flour, yeast, salt and warm water. Cover with a tea towel and leave it somewhere fairly warm for about 10 minutes. Sprinkle with some flour, knead it for 10-20 seconds, cover and leave for the same amount of time. Do this another two times, then knock it into an oval shape, and place it on a floured baking sheet. Cover with a tea towel and leave for about 45 minutes after which it should be about 50-100% bigger

Pre heat your oven to 220°C and place a dish with boiling water on a lower shelf. (This is a top tip for a great crust!)

Dust the loaf with flour and score a cross over the top. Bake 30-40 minutes then remove and let it cool on a rack.

Tip: Feel free to throw a couple of hundred grams of cubed cheddar, pitted olives, crispy bacon, or herbs into the dough.

PASTRY (for savoury pies)
175g Butter
350g Flour
Pinch Salt (only if using unsalted butter)
Water 3-4 tablespoons

Cut butter into cubes and add to flour. Rub using fingertips until mixture appears like fine breadcrumbs. Add cold water such that the mixture becomes a non-sticky dough. Place dough in fridge wrapped in cling film until cool.
On a floured surface, roll out half of the pastry using a rolling pin. Roll away from yourself only for a smoother finish. Use to line a pie dish. Roll out the other half of pastry as a topping.

Tip: Brush with beaten egg to give a "glaze" to the finished pie

BOILED EGG

Bring water to the boil in a pan. Gently place the egg in the water using a spoon, to avoid cracking the shell. Boil for one minute then remove the pan from the heat. Allow the egg to remain in the water for a further 6 minutes, then serve.

Tip: Allow 7 minutes for firmer egg. A hard boiled egg can be made by placing the already boiled egg into cold water for a further 2 minutes.

WHITE SAUCE

425 mls cold milk
20g plain flour
40g Butter

Place milk in saucepan, add flour and butter. Bring to simmering point stirring continuously with a balloon whisk. When the sauce has thickened turn heat down low and cook for 5 minutes stirring occasionally.

CHEESE SAUCE

Make white sauce as above . After simmering for 5 minutes add 75 grams of cheese (you choose!). Season with salt and pepper and whisk until all cheeses melt.

During the 70th Anniversary of the "Dambuster" Raids in May 2013 the Grindleford Schoolchildren raced down to the playing fields hoping to see the last flying Lancaster Bomber. They were rewarded with a spectacular flypast. Photos by Mr Petts.

STARTERS & SNACKS

TOMATO SALAD (by Rosie Jones)
5 tomatoes
10 cm block of cucumber
1 lemons worth of juice
Half a bunch of coriander
Pinch of salt

Slice the tomato. Slice the cucumber. Chop the coriander finely. Put the tomatoes and cucumber mixed with the coriander in a bowl. Sprinkle with the lemon juice and a little salt.
Serve

GRILLED SQUEAKY (HALLOUMI) CHEESE WITH CHERRY TOMATOES (The Heason family)

Serves 4
1 packet of halloumi (250g)
20 cherry tomatoes
1 packet of Halloumi should feed 4 people a reasonable amount of cheese, (but if you are feeling extravagant then get two!). Slice the cheese into half centimetre pieces and grill or dry-fry until brown on each side. Eat whilst still hot with cherry tomatoes.

SMOKED SALMON WITH LEMON JUICE. (The Heason family)

Thinly sliced smoked salmon
1 lemon
Black Pepper
1 lime (optional)
Cream Cheese/Dill sauce (optional)

Lay out individual portions of smoked salmon with lemon or lime wedges. Pepper from a mill and / or Dill Sauce make a nice extra accompaniment. Squeeze lemon/lime juice onto salmon and enjoy.
Tip: If you want to be more sophisticated roll some good quality cream-cheese inside a piece of salmon and eat whole.

"1970'S STYLE" STUFFED MUSHROOMS (The Robertson Family)

6 x Large Field Mushrooms
1 packet dry stuffing mix
6 peeled and chopped Chestnuts (Optional) fresh or vac packed
2 Cloves of garlic - chopped
6 small knobs of butter
Salt and Pepper

Salad leaf garnish

Remove stalk from each of the mushrooms Make stuffing mix as per the packet

Add chopped Chestnuts and garlic to stuffing mix

Put approximately one tablespoon full of stuffing mix into the up-turned mushroom (where the stalk was)

Place a knob of butter on top

Season with salt and pepper

Then place into a hot oven for 10 minutes, until the stuffing top is golden and crispy. Serve with a small salad leaf garnish

Tip: No need to waste the mushroom stalk- just add to stuffing mix. You can also grill these depending on your oven type

CHEESE ON TOAST.

This is a very versatile and mouthwatering snack which can be made in a few minutes. The ingredients may be easy to guess, but the variations are limitless! Any Cheese will do – favourites being Chedder, Mozzarella, Stilton, Edam and Cheshire.

SIMPLE CHEESY TOAST

Two slices of bread – toasted to brown on both sides.

Place thin sliced cheese to cover the toast.

Place under grill (preferable) or microwave until cheese is bubbling.

ADVANCED CHEESY TOAST

Two slices of bread – toasted to brown on both sides

Grate a handful of cheese into a bowl and mix with a desert spoon of milk to a paste.

Spread onto toast and grill. Remove when cheese is bubbling and beautifully browned.

CHEESY TOAST TOPPINGS

Tip: Try the following for variety: Sliced Olives, Capers, Ham pieces, Jalapenos, Black pepper, Henderson's relish (or Worcestershire Sauce). Tomato puree or Pesto can be placed on the toast prior to the cheese if wished.

WELSH RAREBIT

Believed to be a true Welsh Recipe, Welsh rarebit is "Caws Pob" in the Welsh language which means Cheese (Caws) roasted or baked (Pob)

4oz grated, strong cheese such as Cheddar or Cheshire
1/2 tablespoon butter
1 teaspoon Worcestershire sauce
1 level teaspoon mustard

1 teaspoon flour

2 tablespoon beer (or milk)

Pepper to season

2 slices bread toasted on 1 side only

Put the cheese, flour, mustard, Worcestershire sauce, butter and pepper into a saucepan. Mix well and then add the beer or milk to moisten. Do not make it too wet. Stir over a gentle heat until all is melted, and when it is a thickish paste, stop stirring, and swivel it around the saucepan, which it will do quite easily. Leave to cool a little, and meanwhile toast the bread on one side only. Spread the rarebit over the untoasted side and brown under a hot grill.

VEGETARIAN BIRDS NESTS (The Robertson family)

1 large potato, cut into small cubes

2 large carrots, cut into small cubes

$\frac{1}{4}$ of squash or 1 sweet potato, cut into small cubes

2 large heads of broccoli

Butter

Cream

4 Quail Eggs or very small Chicken Eggs

Salt and Pepper

Steam all the veg until soft. Drain the veg then add a knob of butter and add a splash of cream. Mash them up. On a lined tray, divide the mixture into four round shapes. Hollow out the middle so they resemble birds' nests. Place into a hot oven for approx 8 mins, until golden. Remove from oven. Into the hollow of the "Birds' Nests" crack a Quail's Egg

Add a little knob of butter and a splash of cream onto top of Quail's Egg and season with salt and pepper

Place back in the oven for approx 2 mins until egg just cooked

Serve immediately on warm plates

Tip: This is an easy one to do with the kids as they enjoy the mashing bit!

HUMMUS

200g canned chickpeas
2 tbsp lemon juice or more
2 garlic cloves, crushed
1 tsp ground cumin
Salt
100ml tahini (sesame seed paste) optional
4 tbsp water
2 tbsp extra virgin olive oil
1 tsp paprika
4 slices pitta bread

Drain the chickpeas and rinse. Keep a few whole chick peas for serving. Combine the chickpeas, lemon juice, garlic, cumin, salt, tahini, and water in a food processor, and blend to a creamy purée. Add more lemon juice, garlic, cumin or salt to taste. Turn out into a dinner plate, and make smooth with the back of a spoon. Drizzle with extra virgin olive oil and scatter with the spare chickpeas. Sprinkle with paprika and serve with pitta bread, warmed in a moderate oven for three minutes, and cut into quarters.

SMOKED MACKEREL PATE (The Barnett Family)

2 medium smoked mackerel
8oz cottage cheese
Juice $\frac{1}{2}$ lemon
Salt, pepper, grated nutmeg
Lemon wedges to garnish and a pinch of cayenne pepper

Scrape flesh from skin. Flake fish. Add cottage cheese, lemon juice, mix and season. Chill. Garnish with cayenne and the lemon wedges. Serve with toast or warmed pitta bread.

HOT & STICKY SPICED NUTS (The Heason family)

Peanuts or Cashew Nuts
Soy Sauce
Honey
Chilli (fresh powder, or sauce)

Heat together in a frying pan. Stir and toss to coat nuts. Serve whilst hot and sticky.

GRILLED SQUID WITH CHILLIES (by Ayshea Furlong)

6 medium squid, no bigger than your hand
12 large fresh red chillies, seeded and very finely chopped
extra virgin olive oil
sea salt and freshly ground black pepper
3 lemons

Serve with a rocket salad in an oil and lemon dressing.

Clean squid and cut in half by opening up the body to make it flat. Score the inner side of the squid using a serrated knife with parallel lines about 1cm apart and equally the other way to make cross hatching.

Make the sauce - put the chopped chillies in a bowl and cover with about 2.5cm of oil.

Season squid (including tentacles if you have them), with salt and pepper. Place scored side down on a very hot grill for 1 - 2 minutes. Turn the squid pieces over; they will immediately curl up by which time they will be cooked.

Toss the rocket in the oil and lemon dressing. Arrange the squid on the plate, add the rocket and some of the chilli sauce and serve with lemon quarters

GRINDLEFORD

GOURMETS

An anthology of
favourite recipes
by the children,
parents and friends
of Grindleford School

**The cover of the original Grindleford Primary School
Cookbook**

TAPENADE

400g Pitted black olives
75g Capers
50g Tin Anchovy Fillets
2 cloves garlic (crushed)
1 teaspoon Dijon mustard
2 tablespoons olive oil
2 teaspoons lemon juice
2 tablespoons chopped basil
Black pepper

Place all the ingredients into a food processor and mix to a fine paste. Serve with small slices of French bread toast. Tip. Will keep for up to two weeks. Place in a covered jar in the fridge.

SALMON AND ASPARAGUS SALAD
100g Smoked Salmon
125g Asparagus Tips
1 tsp Extra Virgin Olive Oil
2 handfuls of Spinach Leaves
1 handful of Rocket Leaves
50g bean sprouts
4 shallots
2 tomatoes
40g flaked almonds

FOR THE DRESSING:
2 tbsp low-fat mayonnaise
1 tsp lemon juice
1 tsp Worcester Sauce
1 tsp Dijon Mustard
1/2 tsp dried dill
1/2 black pepper

Place asparagus tips in a pan and cover with boiling water. Cook on a medium heat for 8 minutes. Whilst asparagus is cooking, heat the oil in a pan, slice shallots and fry for 2 minutes, then add the bean sprouts. Fry until asparagus is ready. Whilst asparagus is cooking, whisk thoroughly all the dressing ingredients together. Toss spinach and rocket together, and slice tomatoes. Toss bean sprouts and shallots with the spinach and rocket. Place the salad and the tomatoes on the dish. Slice salmon and arrange with asparagus on top of salad. Add dressing and garnish with almond flakes.

Note: This is a variation on one of my Dad's favourite recipes for serving on Christmas Eve!

CROQUE MONSIEUR

This toasted ham and cheese French favourite is a quick supper

2 slices bread
1 tsp mustard
40g grated cheese (Gruyère is recommended)

1 slice ham
15g unsalted butter

Preheat the oven to 180°C. Spread mustard over each slice of bread. Top one of the slices with half the cheese followed by the slice ham. Finish with the remaining cheese on top and sandwich together. Heat the butter in a large frying pan, then add the sandwich and fry for 1-2 minutes on each side, or until golden-brown. Transfer the sandwiches to a baking tray and place into the oven for 4-5 minutes, or until the cheese has melted. Place the sandwich on a serving plate, slice in half and serve immediately.

CROQUE MADAME

Make the Croque Monsieur as above. When serving top with a fried egg and some Béchamel sauce.

CHINESE BEEF DUMPLINGS

Makes about 20 dumplings

For the stuffing

100g beef mince
100g spring onions, thinly sliced
1cmx1cm piece of ginger, thinly chopped
1/2 egg
1 teaspoon sea salt

1 tablespoon dark soy sauce
2 tablespoons water
1 teaspoon sesame oil
1 1/2 tablespoons vegetable oil

For the dough

200g flour
100ml luke warm water

Make the dough by mixing the water and flour. Knead the dough until smooth. The dough should be really soft but not wet. Cover and leave.

Mix remaining the ingredients (except spring onions and ginger) until the meat has a burger-like consistency. Add the spring onions and ginger and mix well.

Place the dough on floured surface, and cut into 4 pieces. Leaving three pieces covered (to prevent drying), take one piece and roll into a sausage about 2cms thick. Cut off a thumb-sized piece of dough from the "sausage", and flatten a small disc. Place the filling in the centre, and nip the sides to make a crescent-shaped dumpling. Continue until all the dough/mixture is used

Place the dumplings for 15 minutes in boiling water. Put 100ml of cold water into the boiling pan after 5 minutes then again after 10 minutes.

Remove from pan and enjoy the hot dumplings with a little Chinese rice vinegar.

MIXED SATAY STICK (by Ayshea Furlong)
12 large raw prawns
350g beef rump steak
1/2 tbsp lemon juice
1 garlic clove peeled and crushed
salt
2 tsp soft dark brown sugar
1 tsp ground cumin
1 tsp ground coriander
1/4 tsp of turmeric
1 tbsp groundnut oil
fresh coriander leaves to garnish

Why I Like Grindleford Primary School.......
"Because you don't have to do anything you don't want to!"
Emily Mottershaw (Year 5)

For the spicy peanut sauce
1 shallot, peeled and very finely chopped
1 tsp demerara sugar
50g creamed coconut
pinch of chilli powder
1 tbsp dark soy sauce
125g crunchy peanut butter

Preheat the grill on high just before required. Soak 8 bamboo skewers in cold water for at least 30 minutes. Peel prawns, leaving tails on. Remove the long black vein along the back of the prawns. Cut the beef into 1cm wide strips. Place the prawns and beef in separate bowls and sprinkle each with 1/2 tbsp of the lemon juice.

Mix together the garlic, pinch of salt, sugar, cumin, coriander, turmeric and groundnut oil to make a paste. Lightly brush over the prawns and the beef. Cover and place in the refrigerator to marinate for 30 minutes, but longer if possible.

Make the sauce. Pour 125ml of water into a saucepan, add the shallot and sugar and heat gently until the sugar has dissolved. Stir in the creamed coconut and chilli powder. When melted, remove from the heat and stir in the peanut butter. Leave to cool slightly then spoon into a serving dish.

Thread 3 prawns on each of the skewers and divide the beef between the remaining skewers. Cook the skewers under a preheated grill for 4-5 minutes, turning occasionally. The prawns should be opaque and pink and the beef browned on the outside but still pink in the centre. Transfer to a warmed dish, garnish with coriander and serve immediately with warm peanut sauce.

CRISPY DEEP FRIED TARANTULAS WITH A LIME AND KAMPOT PEPPER SAUCE (reproduced by kind permission of Friends International)

Don't try this at home!

12 fresh Tarantulas
2 tablespoons white sugar
1 tablespoon salt
8 garlic cloves minced
Sunflower oil for deep frying
For the dip:
4 tablespoons of fresh lime juice
1 tablespoon Kampot Black pepper (or substitute ordinary)
Pinch of salt, pinch of sugar
Red Chillies and Cucumber flowers for garnish

Kill tarantulas by pressing down on their bodies and then remove the fangs. Wash thoroughly. Combine sugar and salt in a little water and marinade the tarantulas for 20 minutes. Heat the sunflower oil and fry garlic until crispy. Remove garlic and set aside. In the same oil fry the spiders for one minute or until crispy.

Place tarantulas on a plate and top with crispy garlic. Garnish with chillies and cucumber flowers and serve with dip on the side.

Friends-International works with children who live and work on the streets offering support, medical care, food and education.

www.friends-international.org

Illustration by Ruby Richardson

39

MAIN COURSES

LAMB DISHES

ROAST LAMB

Best cuts are leg and rack. Lamb can be seasoned with almost anything such as rosemary, oregano, marjoram, thyme, lemon zest, cumin, coriander, mint and garlic; not forgetting salt and pepper alone or in combination with the herbs. The lamb can be seasoned the night before if wished.

Before roasting your lamb, remove it from the refrigerator and allow it to sit for 30 minutes. A piece of meat at room temperature will roast more evenly.

For a lean piece of meat, cook at 230°C for the first 15 minutes, then turn the temperature down to 175C to continue roasting--the meat will take about 60 minutes per kilo to reach medium-rare.

For a fattier piece of meat, roast at 160°C for a longer period of time, allowing the fat to slowly melt and bathe the roast in its own juices. Meat cooked with this method will take about 70 minutes per kilo to reach medium-rare.

Avoid cooking your lamb too much more than this as the meat can become dried out and tough.

Once cooked remove from the oven, place a foil tent loosely over it, and let rest for 15-20 minutes. A well-rested piece of meat will be more tender and retain its juices better when you slice it.

UNCLE CHRIS' AMAZING LAMB CURRY (from the Burn family)

1.2 kg of braising lamb
Few tablespoons of oil
1.5 teaspoons turmeric
1.5 teaspoons cumin
1 teaspoons black mustard seeds
5cm cinnamon stick
2 star anise
5 cardamom pods
1 teaspoon brown sugar
10 curry leaves
1 tin of tomatoes
500mls stock
Fresh coriander

For the chilli paste
1 Onion

5 garlic cloves
4 deseeded chillies (adjust to taste)
3cm piece of ginger
3 tablespoons oil

Make the chilli paste by putting all ingredients in a blender and whizzing up.

Season the meat with salt and pepper.

Heat the oil and gently fry the chilli paste for 30 seconds or so. Add the dry spices, curry leaves and sugar and fry gently for a minute. Add the tomatoes, stock and meat. Cover and very gently simmer for around 4 hours.

Keep checking the meat after 2.5 hours, and when tender remove the lid and continue simmering until the liquid has reduced and thickened slightly.

FOUR SPICES LAMB PIE

One onion
2 cloves garlic
2 tablespoons olive oil
350g Minced Lamb
$\frac{1}{2}$ teaspoon ground cinnamon
$\frac{1}{2}$ teaspoon ground cumin

½ teaspoon ground cloves
Tin of chopped tomatoes (400g)
1 egg
Handful of fresh flat leaf parsley or coriander
Salt and pepper.

For Pastry see "Basics" Section

Chop onion and garlic and fry in olive oil over low heat. Add the lamb and brown. Stir in cinnamon, cumin and cloves. Season with salt and pepper and add tin of tomatoes. Stir and let mixture simmer for 30 minutes. After this time add parsley/coriander. Switch on oven at 220°C. Prepare pastry as in "Basics" section and spoon the mixture into a pastry lined pie dish. Cover the pie with the second circle of pastry and glaze with a beaten egg. Pinch the edges together to make a wavy edge. Bake for 35 minutes until pastry is golden brown.

Tip: Works well with beef mince too!

MORROCAN LAMB TAGINE

2 tablespoons olive oil
1 red onion sliced
1 fennel bulb thinly sliced
2 cloves of garlic thinly sliced
¾ kg lamb cut into thick pieces
1 teaspoon ground ginger

2 teaspoons ground cumin
2 teaspoons ground coriander
$\frac{1}{4}$ teaspoon cayenne pepper
$\frac{1}{4}$ teaspoon salt
150g (1 cup) chopped dates
500ml (2 cups) water

Heat one tablespoon of oil in a tagine base or a casserole dish. Fry onion fennel and garlic until brown. Transfer to a plate and add remaining oil. Fry lamb pieces until browned. Add spices and salt to the meat and stir. Return the vegetables and mix. Add dates and half the water. Cook on a stovetop very gently for 2-3 hours stirring occasionally and adding water if necessary.

SLOW COOKED LAMB IN WINE
1 leg of lamb
2 tablespoons of olive oil
$\frac{1}{2}$ cup of thyme leaves + 1 thyme sprig
$\frac{1}{2}$ cup of rosemary leaves + 1 rosemary sprig
1 bay leaf
1 bottle of red or white wine
4 cloves of garlic
8 shallots
Salt and pepper.

Pre-heat oven to 220°C. Place lamb in a roasting tin and rub with oil salt and pepper. Place in oven for 30 minutes. Remove from oven and reduce oven temperature to 170°C. Spoon off any fat. Place tin over medium heat on stove top, pour in the wine and baste meat. Add thyme leaves, rosemary leaves, garlic and shallots. As soon as the wine boils turn off heat and cover the tin with a foil "tent". Place back in oven for $1\frac{1}{2}$ hours. After this time, carefully remove foil and place back on medium heat to baste the meat again. Add sprigs of rosemary and thyme and the bay leaf. When the liquid boils cover with the foil once more. Return to oven for further $1\frac{1}{2}$ hours. After this remove the meat and allow to rest for 15 minutes. The remaining liquid can be liquidized in a blender to form a delicious gravy. Return the gravy to the stove top and reduce until thickened.

Illustration by Lex Robertson

Liver Stroganoff

1 lb. lambs liver

1½ oz. butter

1½ tablespoon oil

1 onion - thinly sliced

1 clove garlic

8 oz. mushrooms

1½ oz. plain flour

12 fluid ounces of chicken stock

1 tablespoon tomato puree

3 tablespoons of wine or sherry (optional)

salt and pepper

1 tablespoon of parsley

3 tablespoons of soured cream or natural yogurt (optional)

1. Cut liver and onion into thin strips. Fry in oil for 3 - 4 mins.
2. Add garlic and mushrooms. Cook 2 mins. Add flour. Cook 1 min. stirring.
3. Add rest of ingredients except cream. Bring to boil stirring. Cook few mins.
4. Remove from heat. Add cream. If using yogurt then it won't curdle if added on the boil.
5. Serve with rice, pasta or chips.

   Also nice with thin strips of cooked carrot added.

Jennifer Ashton

Recipe from the Old Cookbook by Jennifer Ashton (former teacher at Grindleford Primary School)

PORK DISHES

ROAST PORK

Use a preheated oven at 180°C. For a family of 4-6 use a 1kg joint Then calculate the cooking time: This is 30 minutes for every 500g plus add 30 minutes at the end (for medium)

Dry the rind and score deeply using a sharp knife. Brush with oil (use a vegetable oil not olive) and sprinkle with salt Place on a rack in a roasting tin and open roast in a preheated oven for calculated time (no basting or covering or you will have soft 'crackling' Once cooked, allow the joint to stand (to allow the juices to settle) for 10 minutes before carving

Tip: Make use of the oven while it is on and roast your vegetables at the same time – they will need about 45 minutes Onions can also be scooped out and filled with the meat from your favourite sausages and roasted around the joint (this makes the joint go further too!)

PORK IN CIDER

50g butter
1kg shoulder of pork, cubed
200g streaky bacon, chopped
16 shallots, peeled and left whole
1 small onion, chopped
2 celery sticks, chopped
300ml dry cider

300ml chicken stock
6tbsp crème fraîche
2tbsp cornflour mixed with 2tbsp water
2tbsp Dijon mustard
2tbsp fresh tarragon leaves

Heat the oven to 160 C Heat half the butter in a casserole dish, add half the pork, season and fry for about 10 minutes until thoroughly browned. Remove the meat from the pot with a slotted spoon and reserve. Add the rest of the butter to the casserole and fry the rest of the pork for 10 minutes until evenly browned.
Meanwhile, in another pan, dry-fry the bacon until crispy. Remove, set aside, and then fry the shallots, onion and celery for a few minutes, to soften slightly.
Combine all the pork, the bacon, shallots, onion and celery in the casserole. Pour over the cider and chicken stock to cover. Cover the dish and cook in the oven for 2 hours until the pork is tender.
Add the crème fraîche, cornflour mix, mustard and tarragon to the pan. Heat on the hob and stir until the sauce has thickened slightly

Tip: Put the shallots into a bowl, pour over boiling water and leave for a few minutes. This will help to make peeling them much easier

PORK WITH OLIVE AND PEPPER SAUCE

Preheat the oven to 200°C

4 lean pork loin or leg steaks
4tbsp olive oil
Freshly milled black pepper
Half small onion, finely chopped
1 clove garlic, finely chopped
1 green pepper chopped
1 red pepper chopped
16 black olives, pitted and chopped
200ml vegetable stock
4tbsp fresh basil, chopped

Heat the olive oil in a frying pan. Start by frying the peppers on a low light until just browned and soft; then set aside leaving the oil in the pan. Lightly season the pork with salt and pepper. Cook in the hot oil for 2 minutes on each side. Place on a baking tray. Place the onions and garlic into the pan and cook for 5 minutes to colour slightly, you may need to add a touch of olive oil. Add the peppers and black olives to the frying pan, add the stock and season well. Cook for 15 minutes until slightly thickened then stir in the basil. Return the pork steaks back to the pan and spoon over the sauce. Place the frying pan or transfer to a baking dish and place in the preheated oven Cook for 10-15 minutes to cook through and thicken slightly, do not over cook or the pork will toughen and dry out. Tip: Try these with a little garlic bread.

CREAMY PORK WITH PEPPERS (by Dulcie Jones)

1 Onion
1 vegetable stock cube
1 red Pepper
1 tbsp Oil
1 tsp Oil
2 tbsp plain flour
2 tbsp Soured Cream
Pork Fillet (tenderloin)
3 cloves Garlic

Cut the pork into thin, ~0.8 cm thick, slices. Put the flour in a bag (with no holes), with some salt and pepper. Add the thinly sliced pork to the bag, close firmly and shake to cover all surfaces of the pork with seasoned flour.

Using the tablespoon of oil in a large frying pan with a lid, fry the pork and then set to one side once browned on both sides. Chop the onion, pepper, and crush and chop the garlic. Make up about a pint of stock with stock cube. Add the teaspoon of oil to the pan and add the onion and pepper. Soften for a few minutes with the lid on, then add the garlic, after about a minute add the cooked pork and the stock. Put in a couple of bay leaves if you like. Put the lid on and simmer on a very low heat for about 30 minutes. Take off the heat and stir in the sour cream. Serve with rice.

Illustration by Flynn Codd

CHICKEN DISHES

ROAST CHICKEN

Important: Always wash hands after contact with raw poultry. Always defrost chicken thoroughly. If using stuffing, stuff the neck end only and not the cavity. At the end ensure it is cooked thoroughly (to do this insert a skewer into the thickest part of the leg: if the juices run clear, the chicken is cooked).

Season chicken with salt and pepper. Cook chicken at 220°C for 10 minutes, and then turn the oven down to 190°C. Allow 45 minutes per kg, plus 20 minutes.
Leave the chicken to rest for at least 15 minutes, covered in foil. This allows the juices which have bubbled up during cooking to sink back into the bird, leaving the meat moist

Tips:

1) Stuff the neck cavity only and add this to the total weight before roasting. A halved lemon or onion, or a few fresh herb sprigs in the cavity will add to the flavour.
2) Placing the chicken breast-down in the roasting tin will allow the juices to moisten the breast meat, which otherwise can turn quite dry.

CORONATION CHICKEN
Serves 6

3 lbs Chicken: Cooked, Cold, Skinned and de-boned

The Mayonnaise

1 tbsp Olive oil
1 sm. onion
1 level tbsp Curry powder
1/4 pt stock
1 rounded tsp Tomato purée

Juice of 1/2 lemon
2 rounded tbsp Sweet Chutney
1/2 pt Mayonnaise
3 tbsp Single Cream

Heat oil, chop onion and add to the oil, fry for 5 mins or until soft. add Curry powder and cook for a few minutes. add stock, Tomato purée, strained lemon Juice, chutney. Stir until boiling then Simmer gently for 5 minutes.
   Strain it all into a basin, so there are no lumps. When it is cool stir in the mayonnaise and Cream.
   Put the chicken on a Serving dish in chunky pieces then add the mayonnaise.
   Serve with cold rice salad.

Gillie Jenkinson

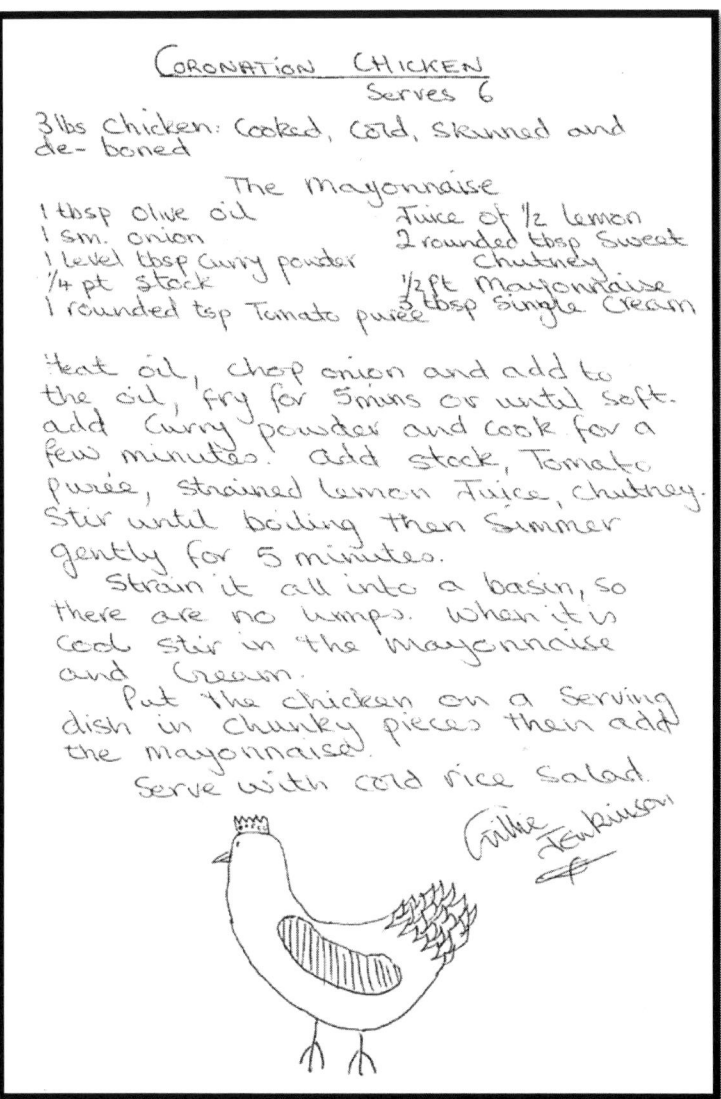

Recipe from the Old Cookbook by Gillie Jenkinson (Gillie's Children Hannah and Ester were former pupils at Grindleford Primary School)

TASTY ROAST CHICKEN AND VEGETABLES (by Samuel Ives)

Serves 4 (if you are very hungry you may need to increase the quantities, but don't overcrowd the roasting tin - use more than one if necessary.)

1 red onion
500g potatoes
2 carrots
olive oil
4 chicken thighs or drumsticks (with skin left on)
1 lemon
1 courgette
1 clove garlic
1 sprig rosemary (optional)

Heat oven to 200°C. Put a large roasting tin in the oven. Cut the onion into wedges and put in a large bowl. Cut the potatoes and carrots into bite-sized chunks. Put them in the bowl and mix in a tablespoon of olive oil. Take the tin out of the oven and lay out the vegetables. Put the chicken on top and add a little pepper. Put in the oven and cook for 20mins. Meanwhile, cut the courgette into 1 cm rounds. Put them in the bowl with the crushed garlic and mix with a tablespoon of olive oil. Cut the lemon into quarters.
Take the tray out of the oven, lift off the chicken, and add the courgettes, lemon and rosemary. Mix to turn the

vegetables then put the chicken back on top and bake for 20-25 minutes.

When cooked the chicken juices should run clear. If pink cook for 10 more minutes and re-test. You may want to squeeze the lemon over your chicken before you eat.

CHICKEN WITH VINEGAR

Very simple and delicious! A traditional French Dish.

1.75kg Chicken (cut into 8 pieces)

150mls Wine Vinegar

Half bottle of Medium-Dry white wine (400ml)

15 shallots

5 cloves of garlic

2 tablespoons olive oil

2 tables spoons of Tarragon Leaves (and some extra to garnish)

Salt and Pepper

2 tablespoons Creme Fraiche

Why I Like Grindleford Primary School.......
"Fun Subjects!"
Archie McMullan (Year 6)

Heat oil in a frying pan (big enough for all the above). Season chicken and fry, removing when browned. Add shallots to now empty pan until brown then add garlic. Reduce heat, return chicken and add tarragon leaves, vinegar and wine until liquid is simmering. Cook for 45 minutes on low heat turning chicken over half way through. Remove chicken, shallots and garlic and place in a serving dish. Add crème fraiche to remaining liquid and whisk, with salt & pepper to taste. Pour sauce over chicken decorating with remaining tarragon leaves.

<u>Chicken with Herbs</u>

Serves 4.

Easy dinner party menu - just keep adding wine!

4 good chicken joints
2 tbs. butter
2 tsp. flour
salt, pepper
6 tbs. white wine
¼ tsp. thyme
¼ tsp. rosemary
1 tbs. chopped parsley.
1 tbs. chopped chives

1. Heat the butter in a thick frying pan, put in the chicken joints + brown all over.
2. Sprinkle with flour + add salt + pepper.
3. Add the wine + herbs.
4. Turn the chicken once or twice and cook over a low heat for about 20 minutes, until chicken is cooked.
5. Correct seasoning, and add more wine if it dries up!

from Sally Turnbull.

Recipe from the Old Cookbook by Sally Turnbull (former pupil at Grindleford Primary School)

POULET EN COCOTTE BONNE FEMME (By Flynn Codd)
Also known as "Posh Sounding Chicken!"

1 chicken (3lbs)
1 tablespoon of olive oil
2 oz butter
8 button onions
6oz diced bacon
4oz button mushrooms
1lb potatoes in small cubes
1 tablespoon chopped chives or parsley
Salt and Pepper

Season Chicken. Heat oil and butter in casserole dish then add chicken to brown. After 5 minutes add onions and bacon. Brown chicken on all sides for a total of 15mins. After chicken is nicely brown add potatoes, mixing well. Cover dish and place in oven at 150°C. Cook for 1hr-1hr30mins. Serve and sprinkle with herbs.

MAPLE ROASTED POUSSIN (by Morgan Strafford)

4 Poussins (Can use 4 chicken breasts)

4 Rosemary Sprigs

4 Garlic cloves peeled and crushed

2 Tablespoons maple syrup

1 Tablespoon Dijon Mustard

2 Tablespoons Olive oil

Ground Black Pepper

Preheat Oven to 200°C. Stuff Poussin (or chicken breast) and loosely tie up with kitchen string. Mix maple syrup, mustard and black pepper. Place Poussin on roasting tray and pour over the syrup mixture. Roast for 40-45 minutes, basting occasionally. Tip: Serve with new potatoes and salad.

GREEK CHICKEN WITH NEW POTATOES AND TOMATOES (By Harry Nicholson)

6 Boneless Chicken Thighs

12-15 New Potatoes
1/2kg Cherry tomatoes
1 tin plum tomatoes
1 tablespoon Oregano
1 Tablespoon Balsamic vinegar
2/3 tablespoon olive oil

Pre-heat oven to 200°C. Bring a pan of water to the boil. Heat Olive oil in pan and brown chicken for 7 minutes. At the same time add potatoes to the boiling water. Add vinegar, olive oil and oregano in a mixing jug. Drain potatoes when soft and add to a baking tray. Lightly crush the potatoes with the back of a spoon. Place chicken on top and cover with tinned tomatoes. Sprinkle mixture on top and bake for 1 hr.

GUMBO (A dish from Louisiana, USA)

4 chicken legs, skin removed
Cayenne pepper
100ml oil
100g flour
1 onion, finely chopped
1 green pepper, finely chopped
1 rib of celery, finely chopped
1 litre chicken stock, at room temperature
Bay leaf
200g okra, chopped

200g smoked sausage, thinly sliced
½ tsp Tabasco, according to taste
Filé powder, to serve (this is ground Sassafras leaves and is optional)

Dust the chicken legs with salt and black and cayenne pepper. Leave to sit for at least half an hour.

Heat the oil in a large, heavy-based pot (not non-stick) over a medium-high heat, and then brown the chicken well, in batches if necessary. Set aside.

Turn the heat down slightly; scrape any bits off the bottom of the pan, then stir in the flour. Stir over a medium-low heat until it reaches a deep, rich, melted milk chocolate shade.

Add the onion, green pepper and celery and cook, stirring for a few minutes until softened. Gradually stir in the stock until you have a smooth sauce, scraping the bottom of the pot as you do so.

Add the chicken and the bay leaf, and bring to a simmer. Turn down, cover and simmer gently for 30 minutes. Add the okra and sausage, stir, replace the lid, and simmer for 45 minutes.

Remove the chicken (keeping the pot on the heat) and, when cool enough to handle, strip the meat from the bones and return to the pot, with Tabasco and salt and pepper to taste. Serve immediately, with long grain rice and filé powder.

Illustration by Saul Robertson

APRITADA (from Painted Plate in Eyam Hall)

This is a chicken and pork stew from the Philippines

Serves 4

4 chicken pieces e.g. thighs/drumsticks - skinned but on the bone
2 pork shoulder steaks - cut into 1inch cubes
1 large baking potato - peeled and chopped
2 to 3 tomatoes - sliced
1 medium onion - diced
1 medium carrot - sliced
1 green pepper cored and cut into strips
2 to 3 cloves garlic
$\frac{1}{2}$ cup dark soy sauce
2 tbsp tomato puree
1 tbsp oil
1 bay leaf
Salt and pepper

Marinate chicken and pork together in dark soy sauce with a good sprinkling of black pepper. Lightly fry garlic in oil until browning. Add onions and fry until opaque. Add tomatoes and toss for 1 min. Add chicken, pork and soy sauce cook for 5 min stirring occasionally. Top up with water and add potato, carrot, tomato puree and bay leaf. Bring to boil and simmer for 45 mins until meat is tender. Add green pepper 5 mins before end of cooking. Add salt and pepper to taste. Serve with plain boiled rice

TIP - Best cooked one day and eaten the next. Alternative recipe – replace the chicken and pork with beef and this becomes 'Mechada'.

Airborne!
Every year the Year 5/6's are taken to the White Hall Outdoor Activity Centre, enjoying a three-day residential visit. Arguably the most popular trip offered, the children have an amazing time as the centre caters for all pupils regardless of ability, experience and confidence.
Photo by Mr Petts.

BEEF RECIPES

ROAST BEEF
2.5kg bone in will feed 6
1.5kg boned will feed 6

The beef should be at room temperature. Stand the beef joint in a roasting tin then cook to the temperature and time as below.

220°C for the first 30 mins then lower the temperature to 190°C for the remaining cooking time then

Rare - 11 mins 450g

Medium - 14 mins 450g

Well done - 16 mins 450g

Once it is removed from the oven the meat must rest. Wrap the meat loosely in aluminium foil and put to one side. 20 minutes should be long enough but up to an hour won't do any harm. The fibres in meat tighten up during cooking and resting allows the fibres to relax, release some of the meat juices (great for the gravy) and results in a soft tender piece of meat. The joint is then ready to carve.

STEAK
You will need a Sirloin, Rib-Eye or Fillet steak.

Allow meat to sit at room temperature for 10 minutes. This is based on a steak approx 1.5cm thick. Slightly fatter or thinner steaks will need more/less cooking time respectively.

Lightly brush each side of the steak with oil and season with salt/pepper. Fry in a very hot heavy based pan for 2 minutes each side to seal in the juices.
Reduce to a medium heat and fry for 4 minutes (rare), 7 minutes (medium) and 11 minutes (well done), turning once. Remove from pan and allow to rest in a warm place for 3-5 minutes.

Tips:
Touch the steak to find out if it's done. It should have spring, but not be limp. If it's firm it's overdone.
Why not try....
Add a knob of butter to the pan and allow to melt. Pour the butter and cooking juices over the steak and serve immediately.

BEEF BOURGUIGNON

Serves 4-6

2 lb (900 g) braising steak, cut into 2 inch (5 cm) squares
3 tablespoons olive oil
1 medium onion, sliced
1 heaped tablespoon plain flour
15 fl oz (425 ml) Burgundy or other red wine

2 cloves garlic, chopped

2 sprigs fresh thyme

1 bay leaf

12 oz (350 g) shallots

225 g streaky bacon, cut into cubes

4 oz (110 g) mushrooms, cut into chunks

salt and freshly milled black pepper

Pre-heat the oven to 140°C

Bring 1 tablespoon of the oil to sizzling point in the casserole or pan and sear the beef, a few pieces at a time, to a rich, dark brown on all sides. Using a slotted spoon, transfer the meat to a plate as it browns. Next add the sliced onion to the casserole and brown that a little too.

Now return the meat to the casserole or pan and sprinkle in the flour, stirring round to soak up all the juices. Then gradually pour in the wine, again stirring all the time. Add the chopped garlic, herbs and seasoning, put the lid on and cook very gently on top of the stove or transfer to the oven - either way it will take 2 hours.

Then, using a bit more olive oil, fry the shallots and bacon in a small frying pan to colour them lightly. Add to the casserole, together with the mushrooms, then put the lid on and cook for a further hour.

BEEF IN BEER

3 fresh or dried bay leaves
500g quality diced stewing beef
500mls stout
2 sticks celery
2 medium onions
2 carrots
Olive oil
1 heaped tablespoon plain flour
400g tinned chopped tomatoes
Salt and black pepper

Pre-heat oven 180°C. (Or you can cook this on a stovetop).
Trim the ends off your celery and roughly chop the sticks.
Peel and roughly chop the onions. Peel the carrots, slice
lengthways and roughly chop.
Put a casserole pan on a medium heat. Put all the vegetables
and the bay leaves into the pan with 2 lugs of olive oil and fry
for 10 minutes. Add your meat and flour. Pour in the stout
and tinned tomatoes. Give it a good stir, then season with a
teaspoon of sea salt (less if using table salt) and a few grinds
of pepper.
Bring to the boil, put the lid on and either simmer slowly on
your hob or cook in an oven for 3 hours. Remove the lid for
the final half hour of simmering or cooking. When done, your
meat should be tender and delicious. Remember to remove
the bay leaves before serving, and taste it to see if it needs
a bit more salt and pepper.

BEEF AND ALE PIE

900g/2lb diced stewing beef
25g/1oz flour, seasoned with salt and freshly ground black
pepper, plus extra for dusting
100g/3½oz butter
2 onions, roughly chopped
2 cloves garlic, roughly chopped
2 medium carrots, roughly chopped
150g/5½oz button mushrooms
2 sprigs fresh thyme
1 bay leaf
400ml/14fl oz good-quality ale
500ml/17fl oz beef stock
salt and freshly ground black pepper
1 free-range whole egg beaten with 1 free-range egg yolk
300g/10½oz ready-made rolled puff pastry

Dip the meat into the seasoned flour, then place a large
lidded pan on the hob. Heat half the butter in the pan and
add the meat. Sear all over until golden brown.

Add the vegetables and herbs, then pour in the ale and stock.
Bring to a simmer, then cover with a lid and gently simmer on
the stove for 1½ hours.

Preheat the oven to 220°C.

Once cooked, season the stew, add the remaining butter and tip into an ovenproof serving dish. Brush the edge of the dish with the beaten egg.

If necessary, roll out the pastry using as little flour as possible and place over the dish. Pinch the edges of the dish so that the pastry will stick to it and trim off any remaining pieces of pastry from around the edge. Cut the leftover pastry into leaves and add them to the top, using the beaten egg as a 'glue', for decoration.

Brush the pastry top thoroughly with the remaining beaten egg and place on a baking tray. Bake in the oven for 20-30 minutes until the pastry is golden brown on top. Serve.

COTTAGE PIE (A traditional English recipe)

1 tablespoon olive oil
1 large onion, chopped
1 clove garlic, crushed
2 medium carrots, chopped
500g beef mince
1 (400g) tin chopped tomatoes
2 tablespoons tomato purée
300ml beef stock
1 teaspoon dried mixed herbs
Dash Worcestershire sauce
Salt and freshly ground black pepper to taste

For the mashed potatoes:
1kg potatoes, peeled and diced
2 teaspoons Dijon mustard
75g butter
4 tablespoons milk

Preheat the oven to 190 C
Heat the oil in a large frying pan over medium high heat. Add the onion, garlic and carrot and cook over a medium heat until soft. Add the mince and cook to brown.
Add the tinned tomatoes, purée, beef stock, mixed herbs and Worcestershire sauce. Season with salt and pepper. Cover and simmer for 30 minutes.
Meanwhile, boil the potatoes in water until soft. Drain and mash with the mustard, butter and milk. Season with salt and pepper.
Spoon the mince mixture into a casserole dish. Top with the mash and bake for 30 minutes until golden brown.

Tip: Replacing the beef mince with lamb mince makes a delicious "Shepherd's Pie"

Grindleford Bridge over the River Derwent and the
Millennium stone – both venues well known to Grindleford
children!

POTATO DISHES

SAUTEED POTATOES
Serves 2

500g small, waxy potatoes (Charlottes are ideal)
1 tbsp olive oil (for oil, add a knob of butter at the end of cooking)
1 clove of garlic, finely chopped
2 tbsp chopped parsley, tarragon and chives
Knob of butter

Put the potatoes in a pan of well-salted cold water and bring to the boil. Simmer for 15 minutes (depending on size) until tender. Drain well, and return to the hot pan to steam for a couple of minutes.
When cool, cut into 5mm slices. Heat the oil in a pan over medium heat and add the potatoes in a single layer (in batches if necessary). Season and cook undisturbed until golden brown. Flip over, repeat.

Add the garlic and butter to the pan and sauté briefly, then drain on kitchen paper, scatter with the herbs and serve immediately.

Why I Like Grindleford Primary School.......
"Playing on all the computers!"
Nathan Gilbert (Year 5)

POTATOES BOULANGERE

Pre-heat the oven to gas 180°C.

1.25kg Desirée or Romano potatoes, peeled

10g fresh rosemary

2 medium onions, peeled

275ml vegetable stock

150ml milk

40g butter

sea salt and freshly milled black pepper

Strip the stalks from the rosemary.
After that, take two-thirds of the leaves and chop them
finely. Now cut the onions in half and then the halves into the
thinnest slices possible; the potatoes should be sliced, but
not too thinly.
Arrange a layer of potatoes, then onions, in the dish, followed
by a scattering of rosemary, then season. Continue layering in
this way, finishing with a layer of potatoes that slightly
overlap.
Now mix the stock and milk together and pour it over the
potatoes. Season the top layer, then scatter over the whole
rosemary leaves. Put little flecks of the butter all over the
potatoes and place the dish on the highest shelf of the oven
for 50-60 minutes, until the top is crisp and golden.

POTATOES DAUPHINOISE
Serves 6

30g butter
1kg floury potatoes
400ml double cream
2 large garlic cloves, crushed
$\frac{1}{4}$ teaspoon freshly grated nutmeg
Sea salt and freshly ground black pepper

Preheat the oven to 160°C. Rub a gratin dish liberally with the butter. Peel the potatoes and slice them thinly. In a large bowl, whisk together the cream, garlic and nutmeg and season well with salt and pepper. Toss the potatoes in the creamy mixture, then layer them in the gratin dish, spreading them as flat and evenly as you can. Pour over any remaining cream. Bake for $1\frac{1}{4}$-$1\frac{1}{2}$ hours, pressing down with a spatula every 15 minutes or so to compress the potatoes and stop them drying out. The gratin is ready when the top is golden and bubbling and the potatoes are tender. You may want to turn the oven up to 200°C for the last 5 minutes to achieve a bit of extra bubbling crispness. Leave to stand for 5 minutes or so before serving.

CEPELINAI (By Daiva Bernotaitis)
These are Lithuanian potato dumplings.

2kg potatoes

Pinch of salt
1 pound minced pork
1 egg
1 onion
For the Sauce:
1 onion
Bacon or mushrooms
200 ml double cream
Salt + pepper

Peel and boil 500g of potatoes, then mash it and set aside.
Peel the rest of potatoes and finely grate them. Using a clean
large cloth squeeze the juice out of grated potatoes (a little
at a time). Leave the juice in a bowl for 5 min, the starch will
set at the bottom, pour liquid away but keep the starch. Mix
grated potatoes, mash potatoes and the starch together, add
some salt. It should look like dough.
Finely chop the onion and mix with minced meat and one egg,
add some salt and pepper.
Take a ball of potato dough and flatten it in your palm, put
one spoon of meat mixture in the middle and fold potato
dough around, making an oval shape dumpling and set aside.
Repeat until you run out of dough.

Boil a big pot of water, add a pinch of salt. Once water is boiling, put dumplings into it. Let it boil again, then reduce the heat and boil for 15-20 min, mixing occasionally.

Now prepare the sauce. Finely chop onion and fry it on a low flame with some oil for about 5 min, then add bacon or mushrooms and fry for a bit longer. Finally pour cream in, mix and set aside.

Put 2 dumplings on the plate, pour 2-3 spoons of sauce on top and serve. Enjoy.

HOMITY PIE (from The Tideswell School of Food)

For the Wholemeal savoury short crust pastry

- 250g cold butter, diced
- 500g plain flour
- 500g wholemeal flour
- 50g mixture of poppy seeds, sesame seed, sunflower seeds
- 250g cold white vegetable fat (trex, flora)
- Enough water to form a soft but not sticky dough, about 250ml

In a food processor or by hand, rub the two fats into the flour until they become fine breadcrumbs. Add the seeds. Using a table knife gradually add the water bit by bit until the dough comes together, knead lightly and form into a ball and ensure that the fat is evenly distributed. Divide into two balls and chill in the fridge for 30 mins. Roll the pastry out to about 5mm thickness and use it to line a spring form cake tin that has been greased and floured. Push the pastry gently into the edges and corners and leave an overlap of pastry or about 2 cm to allow for shrinkage.

For the Homity Pie Filling

500g cooked potatoes

1 large white onion

1 clove of garlic

1 teaspoon dried thyme

Salt and black pepper

2 tablespoons chopped fresh flat leaf parsley

150g mature cheddar cheese

1 tablespoon whipping or double cream

1 knob of butter

Finely slice the onion and garlic. In a frying pan melt the butter and add the onion, cook for 10 mins until soft and sweet, add the garlic and cook for another 5 minutes until the onions are just turning golden around the edges.

Remove from the heat and place in a large bowl.

Add the potatoes, herbs, cream and most of the cheese, salt and plenty of black pepper, mix really well together crushing some of the potatoes up and leaving some in large chunks.

Spoon the mixture into the pastry case and top with the rest of the cheese. Place in oven at 180°C on the middle shelf and cook for 40 minutes to 1 hour.

Remove from the oven when the pastry is crisp and golden and stand for 10 mins. Slide the pie from base onto a plate, slice a big wedge and serve with crisp green salad.

Illustration by Holly Luscombe

PASTA DISHES

VEGETARIAN PASTA

100g cooked chestnuts
Handful each basil, parsley and mint , leaves only

50g Parmesan, grated, plus extra to serve (optional)
2 garlic cloves
150ml rapeseed oil
500g dried pasta
1 tbsp olive oil
250g pack chestnut mushrooms , quartered

Put the chestnuts in a food processor and pulse until roughly chopped. Throw in the herbs, Parmesan and garlic, then pulse again until chopped (not too finely). Pour in the rapeseed oil, mix together and season to taste.
Cook the pasta in plenty of boiling salted water, according to pack instructions. Meanwhile, heat the olive oil in a large frying pan and fry the mushrooms with some seasoning for 6-8 mins until tender and starting to brown. When the pasta is cooked, drain it, return to the pan, and then stir through the chestnut mix and the mushrooms. Serve with some extra Parmesan on top, if you like.
Tip: **Roasting fresh chestnuts.** For this recipe, either buy a pack of vacuum-packed ready-cooked chestnuts, or roast them yourself. Cut a small cross in each whole chestnut and

roast at 200°C for 30 mins. Remove and allow to cool slightly before crushing with the flat side of a knife

SPAGHETTI BOLOGNESE
(By Oscar Dobson "Blumenthal")
Serves 4
Preparation 15 minutes
Cooking time 1 hour

400g of mince
1 onion finely chopped
1 red pepper finely chopped
1 clove garlic crushed
700g of passata
200ml of beef stock
375g of spaghetti
Grated parmesan to serve on top

Fry the onion in a large frying pan until clear then add the garlic. Add the mince and stir until the meat is browned. Add the passatta and the pepper. Finally, add the stock and stir everything together. Turn down the heat and let the whole concoction simmer for 1 hour.
Turn off the heat from under the Bolognese and add the spaghetti to a huge pan of boiling water and make sure the spaghetti is completely submerged. Gently boil for 12 minutes (or whatever it says on the packet). Drain and add a splash of olive oil and cover the spaghetti with it.

Serve the spaghetti into the bowl and spoon the sauce onto the top of the pasta.
Sprinkle the grated parmesan on the top and serve with a glass of Ribena.

TAGLIATELLE CARBONARA (By Ezri Petts)
To serve 4

350g dried tagliatelle
150g streaky bacon
50g Parmesan cheese
3 medium eggs
3 tablespoons of single cream
2 cloves of garlic
2 tablespoons of chopped fresh parsley
Olive oil
Salt and pepper

Cut the rind off of the bacon and slice into strips (using scissors is easier) and put into a pan. Peel (but don't crush, it's just for flavour) the garlic and add it to the pan with 1 1/2 tablespoons of olive oil. Cook over a medium heat for 3-4 mins until the bacon is crisp. Turn off the heat and remove the bacon onto some kitchen roll to drain the fat. Throw away the garlic. Break the eggs into a bowl. Add the cream, pepper, chopped parsley and half of the cheese (finely grated) and mix with a fork. Boil a saucepan of salted water (with a teaspoon of olive oil). Add the tagliatelle and cook it for as long as it says on the pack. When the pasta is cooked, drain it and put it back in the pan. Add the bacon to the pasta, then the egg mixture, and stir well until there is no liquid egg left. Spoon out into four bowls and sprinkle the remaining cheese over the top.

SPAGHETTI MILANESE (from Andrew Lawton, Furniture designer and maker, Grindleford)

Serves 2
200g spaghetti
1 onion
1 tin chopped tomatoes
25g butter
100g mature cheddar cheese
1 tablespoon flour
Milk

Finely chop the onion and add it to half the butter melted in a saucepan. Cook for a few minutes. Add the tomatoes and season. Cook for 20 minutes. Boil the spaghetti for 12 minutes. When spaghetti is ready make a cheese sauce (see "Basics" but you'll have to reduce the quantities a little) and add it to the onions and tomatoes. Drain the spaghetti add to the rest, mix well and serve.

THE CRUTCHLEY FAMILY MACARONI CHEESE (The original comfort food!)

Macaroni
Milk
Cheese (cheddar is by far the best)
Mustard
Plain Flour
Salt and pepper

Preheat your oven to 180°C. Boil a large pan of water with a pinch of salt and a dash of olive oil added. Grate a handful of cheese per person. Add 100g of macaroni per adult and 50g per child to the boiling water and cook according to packet instructions (usually 10 to 12 minutes). Make sure you give the macaroni a stir to stop it sticking to itself and the bottom of the pan. While the macaroni is cooking make the cheese sauce.

Melt 15g of butter per person in a saucepan over a medium heat. When the butter is melted add one heaped tablespoon of flour per person and stir with a wooden spoon to combine. Cook for a minute stirring constantly to form a smooth paste.

To the paste add $\frac{1}{4}$ of a pint of milk per person plus $\frac{1}{2}$ a teaspoon of English mustard, a pinch of salt and a couple of grounds of pepper. Stir constantly with a hand whisk until the sauce thickens and just begins to bubble. It's important to bring the sauce to a slow bubble to ensure it doesn't taste floury.

The sauce should be thick (i.e. like a thick custard). If too thick add a little pasta water. Take the sauce off the heat and whisk in about $\frac{3}{4}$ of the cheese until it is melted and combined.

Drain macaroni and return to pan, stirring in $\frac{3}{4}$ of the cheese sauce. Grease a Pyrex dish with butter or olive oil, and add macaroni and sauce mixture. Add remaining sauce to top to completely cover macaroni (this stops any of the macaroni going hard in the oven). Sprinkle the rest of the cheese evenly on top. Bake for 15 minutes (or until the top has browned).

When it is done, take it out of the oven and leave it for about 5 minutes. This makes it slightly cooler, but also will ensure it is not too sloppy when you serve it.

Macaroni cheese tips:
1) You can serve it with a side salad but to be honest, it's nicer on its own. Have some fruit afterwards instead.

2) For a healthier version of this dish you could use olive oil and skimmed milk and reduced fat cheese, but frankly, what's the point? It's comfort food. (n.b. if you decide to use reduced fat cheese, bear in mind that any cheese with more than 30% reduced fat will not melt properly on top of the dish)

SUPER SPEEDY SUPPER (LOVE IT OR HATE IT?)
By Archie and Bertie McMullan

Pasta - any shape but Fresh Tagliatelle is best.
1 tablespoon Marmite
1 oz Butter

Cook the pasta as per instructions, until al dente. Drain the pasta - reserving a little of the cooking liquid (2tbs). Whilst the pasta is in the colander place the butter in the hot pan and melt. Stir the marmite in to the butter to make a sauce. Add the cooking liquid to thin the sauce. Return the pasta to the pan and stir into the sauce. Enjoy!!!!

"MUMMY, CAN I HAVE SOME MORE?" PASTA SAUCE
(by Madelina Richardson)

1 onion
2 cloves of garlic
1 medium aubergine and 1 medium courgette
1 carton of passata
250g mascarpone cheese

Fry onions and garlic until soft
Add courgettes and aubergine
Add passata and simmer for 45 mins
Wait to cool and then blend until very smooth
Add mascarpone cheese and heat until melted.

Try.....

Add to tortellini and add freshly milled black pepper and grated cheese.

Great to make in batches and freeze!

ENZO'S MEATBALLS AND SPAGHETTI (Jakey's favourite tea)

500g of lean beef mince.
1 tablespoon parsley
1 tablespoon basil
4 spring onions (chopped)
Zest of 1 lemon (honestly - it makes all the difference!)
1 carrot (finely grated)
100g breadcrumbs
A pinch of ground cinnamon
Salt and freshly ground black pepper
A little olive oil
Tomato sauce to serve with them (or use recipe below).
400g spaghetti
Freshly grated parmesan cheese

Put a large pan of water on to boil. Put the mince in the bowl with the spring onions, lemon zest, carrot, bread crumbs and cinnamon. Now for the messy bit!

Mix it all together with your hands and season well.

Take walnut-sized pieces of mince mixture and roll into balls. (At this point you can freeze any you won't use, as long as the meat was not frozen previously).

Heat a little olive oil in a pan and fry the meatballs lightly until golden.

Heat the sauce in a pan and add the meatballs.

Meanwhile, cook the spaghetti in the boiling water until al-dente.

Add a ladle full of pasta water to the sauce and meatballs, this will loosen the mixture and help bring all the flavours together.

Drain the pasta well, return it to the pan and add the meatballs and sauce.

Toss everything together and serve.

MAMA J's MEATBALLS (By Lex and Saul Robertson)

1 onion

4 cloves garlic

1 red pepper

1 courgette

1 tin of tomatoes

1 pack of fresh meatballs (or use recipe above)

1 pack spaghetti

Grated Cheese

Chop all fresh ingredients and place in oven dish. Add meatballs. Pour tin of tomatoes over all ingredients. Put in oven at 180°C for 25-30 minutes. Serve with spaghetti and grated cheese.

QUICK PASTA SAUCE (by Ruth Capper)

1 small onion, chopped
1 clove garlic, crushed
3-4 rashers bacon, chopped
5-6 mushrooms
1/2 courgette, chopped
Oregano
Small tub creme fraiche
Parmesan
Black pepper

Why I Like Grindleford Primary School.......
"They do great clubs."
Benny Crowson (Year 6)

Cooking Instructions: Fry onion until soft and translucent. Add garlic and bacon and cook until bacon is browned. Add mushrooms and courgette, sprinkle over oregano. When vegetables have softened, add creme fraiche and allow to melt. Add parmesan and black pepper taste.

Serve with pasta, such as penne.

Mother's Egg-slicer

I don't believe she ever used it.

I did, loved the guillotine precision

of eight wires through hard-boiled egg,

perfect discs spaced on buttered bread,

but more, the way each wire

plucked a different note, a scale

nobody had heard before, strummed

arpeggios that tuned the ear far away,

to blue silk kimonos like the one

my uncle brought back from the east,

the hobbled steps of tiny feet, the flirt

of painted fans, or the eggshell china

light shone through, a dragon's egg,

a dance of something yet unhatched.

Ann Atkinson
Reproduced with the kind permission of her daughters,
Rosie & Holly.
(See also Page 11)

EGG DISHES

SCRAMBLED EGGS - PER PERSON (by Carlos)

2 large eggs
1 tablespoon of milk
1 tablespoon of butter
Pinch of salt

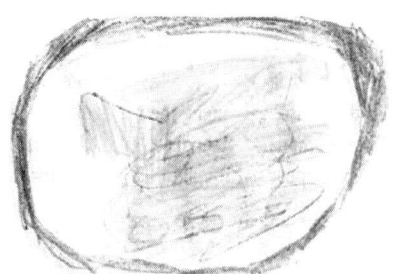

Using a fork mix the eggs and milk together in a bowl. Season with salt and stir. Melt the butter in a medium saucepan. Add the mixture of the eggs and cook gently, stirring, until the eggs are scrambled.

SPANISH OMELETTE

4 large potatoes
1 large red onion, finely sliced
2 red peppers thinly sliced
2 tablespoons of oil
6 medium eggs
Large handful of chopped fresh herbs (whatever you like!)

Preheat the grill. Peel and cut potatoes into chunks and boil until just tender. Fry onion and peppers in the oil until soft.

Add potatoes and mix. Crack the eggs into a bowl and whisk with herbs. Pour the egg mix over the potato mix and simmer gently until the bottom of the mixture is cooked. Place under grill and cook the top.

Slice into wedges and serve with salad.

EGG FRIED RICE (by Dulcie Jones)

200g basmati rice
2 onions
4 eggs
Pinch of salt
2 tablespoons of oil

Cook the rice in twice its volume of water with the salt for 13 minutes. Ideally this should be done in advance so that the rice has chance to cool. Chop the onion. Break the eggs into a jug and whisk with a fork. Heat the oil in a large frying pan and fry the onions until caramelised. Add the rice and stir for a minute. Pour in the egg whilst continue to stir until the egg is cooked. Serve immediately. Some people may like to add soy sauce at the table.

A MAP OF GRINDLEFORD by

by Bryn Heason april 2 2012

KEY
1. My house
2. Our garden
3. the allotments
4. Cath's house
5. Garage
6. School
7. Sir William
8. Sports Field
9. playground
10. church
11. SWP Close?
12. art gallery

Hathersage

Sheffield

this map is not to scale

Grindleford School during a visit to the
English Institute of Sport

Discovering Science

FISH DISHES

HAZEL'S FAVOURITE 'FISH IN PASTRY' (by Hazel Platts)

One large piece of fresh salmon (approx 4oz portion but size to suit appetites)
One pack of ready to roll puff pastry
1oz butter
Freshly chopped herbs (a mixture of parsley, dill and chives is good)
Salt and fresh black pepper
One beaten egg to glaze

Remove the skin and brown fish from the underside. Make sure that all the bones are removed too. Mix the fresh herbs with the butter. Make small cuts into the flesh of the fish and push the herb butter into the cuts. Season the top of the fish with salt and fresh black pepper to taste.

Roll out the puff pastry or use ready rolled pastry to encase the fish, make sure the edges are well sealed with beaten egg or dampened with water. Brush the pastry with beaten egg to glaze during cooking. Any off cuts of pastry can be used to decorate! Carefully lift onto a baking sheet and bake at gas mark 6 or 200°C for about 30 minutes until golden brown. Hazel loves this served with hollandaise sauce, new potatoes and baby vegetables.

MUMMY`S FISHY CAKES (By Emily Barnett)

2 smoked mackerel fillets
4 middle size potatoes
Little flour
Little butter
1 egg
1 tablespoon fresh chopped parsley
1 squeeze lemon
Salt and pepper to taste

For the Sauce:

2 tablespoons natural yoghurt
1 tablespoon mayonnaise
1 teaspoon chilli sauce
Little pepper

Cook and mash the potatoes. Then break up the fish.
Mix potatoes, fish, butter, egg, parsley and lemon and make
into balls. Put into some tins (with flour in). Cook until ready.

Mix all ingredients for sauce together and serve with cooked
fishcakes.

TUNA FISH PASTIES

INGREDIENTS

2 TINS TUNA
1 LEMON JUICE
PUFF PASTRY
$\frac{1}{4}$ PINT WHITE SAUCE

METHOD

ROLL PASTRY IN TO 5" ROUNDS
BRUSH WITH BEATEN EGG
BAKE EITHER GAS 7 ELECTRIC H25° 15-20 MINS.
MAKE WHITE SAUCE
DRAIN EXCESS LIQUID OF TINS OF TUNA FLAKE
AND ADD TO WHITE SAUCE WITH LEMON JUICE
ADD A LITTLE PEPPER

SPLIT COOKED PASTRY CASE AND FILL WITH TUNA
MIXTURE ADD A SLICE OF TOMATO.

RETURN TO OVEN TO WARM THROUGH.

THESE CAN BE EATEN HOT OR COLD.

Recipe from the Old Cookbook by Janet Harby (former Cook at Grindleford Primary School)

DAD'S DELICIOUS RISOTTO (by Holly Luscombe)

1 table spoon of oil
1/2 cup of frozen peas
1/2 cup of chopped carrots
500mls vegetable stock
1 cup of risotto rice
One onion chopped (optional)
One clove garlic (optional)

Heat oil in saucepan then add rice and carrots. Add half of the vegetable stock and bring to the boil. Turn down to simmer, keep adding stock as it gets dry. Add frozen peas 5 minutes before serving. When rice is soft it is done!

Tips: Fry chopped onion and garlic at start if wished. Great camping food!

NAAN BREAD

150ml hand-hot milk
2 tsp caster sugar
2 tsp dried active yeast
450g plain flour
$\frac{1}{2}$ tsp salt
1 tsp baking powder
2 tbsp vegetable oil, plus a little extra
150ml natural yogurt
1 large egg, lightly beaten

Put the milk in a bowl. Add 1 tsp of the sugar, and the yeast. Stir to mix. Set aside for 15-20 minutes or until the yeast has dissolved and the mixture is frothy.

Sift the flour, salt and baking powder into a large bowl. Add the remaining 1 tsp sugar, the yeast mixture, 2 tbsp vegetable oil and the yogurt and egg. Mix and form a ball of dough.

Empty the ball of dough on to a clean surface and knead it for 10 minutes or more, until it is smooth and satiny. Form into a ball. Pour about 0.25 tsp oil into a large bowl and roll the ball of dough in it. Cover the bowl with a piece of cling film and set aside in a warm, draught-free place for an hour or until the dough has doubled in bulk.

Pre-heat your oven to the highest temperature. Put the heaviest baking tray you own to heat in the oven. Pre-heat your grill.

Punch down the dough and knead it again. Divide into 6 equal balls. Keep 5 of them covered while you work with the sixth. Roll this ball into a tear-shaped naan, about 25cm in length and about 13cm at its widest. Remove the hot baking tray from the oven and slap the naan on to it. Put it immediately into the oven for 3 minutes. It should puff up. Now place the baking tray and naan under the grill, about 7.5-10cm away from the heat, for about 30 seconds or until the top of the naan browns slightly. Wrap the naan in a clean tea towel. Make all the naans this way and serve hot.

MINI TOADS
****

You will need:-

1/2 lb small sausages
4 oz plain flour
1 egg
1/2 pint of milk
pinch of salt

a bun tin or small yorkshire pudding tins
Heat oven to 218°C

Put a little oil and one small sausage in each bun tin and place in oven.

Meanwhile add the salt to the flour and stir in the egg and a little of the milk. Gradually add the rest of the milk stirring all the time and making sure there are no lumps. Half fill each bun tin with the mixture and return to the oven for approximately 20 mins.

David Wood

Recipe from the Old Cookbook by David Wood (former pupil at Grindleford Primary School)

SAUSAGE BAKE

3 large potatoes, sliced
1 onion, sliced
$\frac{1}{2}$ small red cabbage, sliced
4 large pork sausages
1 tsp mixed herbs
Salt and pepper
$\frac{1}{2}$ pint gravy (made from Bisto/Oxo)

Pre-heat oven to 170°C

Put two thirds of the sliced potatoes and the sliced onion into a casserole dish, cover with the sliced red cabbage.

Brown the sausages, then cut each into four. Add to the casserole, then cover with the remaining sliced potatoes. Sprinkle over the mixed herbs and season. Pour over the gravy. Cover and cook for about $2\frac{1}{2}$ - 3 hours.

Serves two, easily doubled.

SOUPS & SAUCES

THE BARNETT`S BRILLIANT BROCCOLI (AND STILTON) SOUP

A splash of oil
1 onion
1 large broccoli
1.5 litres of chicken or vegetable stock
200 gm of stilton cheese
Salt and pepper to taste

Chop the onion and fry it in the oil using a large pan then add the stock. Chop the broccoli roughly and add it to the liquid. Boil for about 20 minutes then liquidise the broccoli. Roughly chop up the stilton and add this to the liquid. When this has melted the soup is ready – just add salt and pepper to taste.

PS You can use a strong cheddar if stilton is not liked by everyone.

MUMMY'S MINESTRONE (by Adam Harby)

75g spaghetti, broken into pieces
1 large onion
2 sticks celery

2 carrots
2 potatoes
Handful of frozen peas
1 tsp mixed herbs
1¾ pints vegetable stock
Can of chopped tomatoes
1 tbsp tomato puree
Pinch of sugar
Salt and pepper
Grated cheese
You can add any vegetable you have, e.g. sweet corn, courgettes, even a tin of beans is a good addition.

Cook the pasta in a separate pan. Drain and set aside. Chop the vegetable into bite sized chunks. Heat the olive oil in a large pan. Fry onion until golden and softened. Add all vegetables except peas. Add herbs and stir well. Pour in the stock and chopped tomatoes, sugar and tomato puree. Bring to the boil, stirring occasionally. Don't let the vegetables stick to the bottom of the pan! Turn the heat to low and simmer for approximately 15minutes or until the vegetables are tender. Add frozen peas and pasta and make sure thoroughly heated through. Season with salt and pepper. Ladle into bowls and garnish with grated cheese.

PEA SOUP (By Amelie Cannell)

2 tablespoons olive oil
1 tablespoon butter
1 small onion
1 clove garlic
$\frac{1}{2}$ teaspoon ground pepper
700g frozen peas
800mls vegetable stock
Sprig fresh mint
Cream (optional)

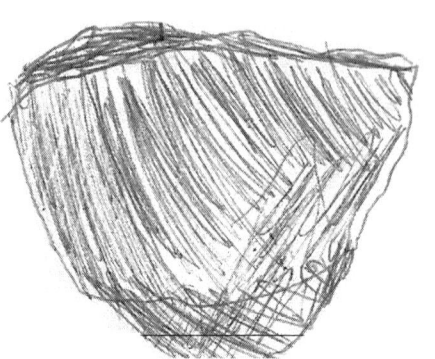

Finely chop the onion and crush the garlic. Fry gently in melted butter and oil. Add frozen peas and continue to fry gently until peas are thawed – then add vegetable stock. Add pepper and puree the soup in a blender with the mint leaves. Warm through and serve with a whirl of cream.

MISO SOUP (By the Robertson family)
"Monday Night, Miso Night" (Serves 4)

Bunch of spring onions, snipped in half
Generous handfuls :-
       Mushrooms, sliced
       Broccoli, mini-trees
       Carrots, sliced
       Pepper, sliced in lengths

Or any veg you wish to use –
Courgette, Aubergine, Chard etc.

4 Cloves of Garlic, chopped
½ teaspoon of dry flaked Chilli

Any leftover cooked meat from your Sunday roast. Chicken /
Beef/ Pork - cut into strips
Handful of raw watercress or raw spinach leaves, per bowl
4 x Miso soup paste
1 packet of Sobu / Udon noodles or egg noodles

Add all veg into a large hob cooking pot and heat on stove.
Stir for 2 mins. Then add garlic and chilli and meat and stir
for 30 seconds. Then pour 4 cupfuls of water in, lid on – bring
up to boil. Simmer for 5 minutes.
At the same time bring your noodles up to boil in another pan.
When noodles are cooked (approx. 5 mins) drain then put into
the cooking pot with all your veg and meat.
Take off heat and stir in Miso Soup Paste, then serve in
bowls, with a topping of Watercress/ Spinach.
Tip: It is a very splashy and slurpy dish, so napkins are
essential!

*Why I Like Grindleford Primary
School.......
"Because it's small"
Emily Barnett (Year 5)*

WILD MUSHROOM CAPPUCCINO (from Eyam Hall Buttery)

Here's a nice little recipe for a soup with a difference that featured in the Sheffield Telegraph Eating Out Food Guide on 17th June 2007 and remained on our Greek Heaven Menu for some time.

Serves 4
Cappuccino

60gms/2oz butter
2 tbsp olive oil
240gms/4oz wild mushrooms
4 cloves of garlic
600mls/1pt chicken or vegetable stock
150mls/$\frac{1}{4}$pt double cream
$\frac{1}{4}$tsp grated nutmeg
Salt & black pepper to season

Garlic Toast
1 crusty French stick
60gms/2oz butter
2 cloves of garlic
1tsp chopped fresh parsley

To make the soup, gently heat the butter and olive oil in a saucepan until the ingredients start to go frothy.

Add the finely chopped garlic and roughly chopped mushrooms and gently cook for 3 minutes.

Add the warm stock, bring to the boil and gently simmer for 6 minutes until the mushrooms are tender.

Whilst the soup is simmering, gently melt the butter in a frying pan, add the finely chopped garlic and gently cook for 30 seconds, add 1.25cms/$\frac{1}{2}$ inch thick slices of bread and gently fry for 30 seconds on each side until golden brown and then place onto a piece of kitchen towel on a warm plate and keep warm.

When the soup is cooked, add the nutmeg, double cream and season to taste, then using an electric hand-whisk, whisk the top of the soup until frothy.

Serve immediately with side portions of garlic toast.

Tomato, Apple and Celery cream soup.

1 pint chicken stock,
4 g onions finely chopped.
5-6 g tomatoes, quartered using stalks as well!
5-6 g apples quartered using cores as well!
5-6 g celery cut into 2 inch lengths - leaves as well!
2 g butter
2 ½ fluid g dry sherry
¼ tsp salt + freshly milled black pepper.
Freshly grated nutmeg
1 small pinch ground ginger.

Melt butter + cook onion gently until golden (10 mins)
Add sherry, vegetables, fruit, spices and seasonings
to pan, turning over the ingredients so evenly coated.
Place double thickness of dampered greaseproof
paper over the ingredients + cover pan with lid.
Simmer very gently for 1 hour, checking that
nothing is sticking.
Add stock to contents of pan (first removing
paper!) and stir well.

Liquidise then sieve to remove pips + chalk etc.
and return to a clean pan.
Reheat, check seasoning, ladle into warmed soup
bowls and garnish with apple slices and snipped
chives.

Alison Whiteley.

Recipe from the Old Cookbook by Alison Whiteley (Former PTA Member for Grindleford Primary School)

FRENCH ONION SOUP

Serves 4-6
6 large onions, peeled and thinly sliced
Olive oil
1/4 teaspoon of sugar
2 cloves garlic, minced
8 cups of beef stock
1/2 cup dry white wine
1 bay leaf
1/4 teaspoon of dry thyme
Salt and pepper
8 slices of toasted French bread
$1\frac{1}{2}$ cups of grated Swiss Gruyere

In a large saucepan, sauté the onions in the olive oil on medium high heat until well browned, but not burned, about 30-40 minutes (or longer). Add the sugar about 10 minutes into the process. Add garlic and sauté for 1 minute.

Add the stock, wine, bay leaf, and thyme. Cover partially and simmer for 30 minutes. Season to taste with salt and pepper. Discard the bay leaf.

To serve, place in large casserole dish. Cover with the toast and sprinkle with cheese. Place in oven 10 minutes at 180°C until the cheese bubbles/browns. Serve immediately.

PEPPER SAUCE FOR STEAK

2.5ml/½tbsp vegetable oil
1 small onion, peeled and finely chopped
150ml/5fl oz dry white wine
150ml/5fl oz crème fraîche or double cream
2 tbsp green peppercorns, rinsed
Salt and freshly ground black pepper to season

Heat the oil in a small frying pan and gently cook the onion
until soft. Add the wine and reduce by half.
Stir in the crème fraîche and the peppercorns.
   Season with salt and plenty of freshly ground black pepper

Illustration by Sydney Codd

JAM & MARMALADE

JAM AND MARMALADE TIPS

You need a large, wide, deep pan to make your jam or marmalade. This helps the liquid evaporate quicker and reduces the likelihood of the jam/marmalade boiling over. The mixture should not come any higher than halfway up the sides.

For marmalade the pectin (the natural substance that sets the marmalade) is found in the pips and pith, which is why they are boiled with the marmalade. It's important to let the marmalade stand for about 20 minutes before putting into jars, to distribute the zest evenly.

Finally, as with all preserves, jars need to be sterilised first. To sterilise the jars: Preheat the oven to 120°C/fan 100°C/gas $\frac{1}{2}$. Wash the jars in warm soapy water, rinse in clean water and place on a tray in the oven for about 10 minutes. After placing the jam/marmalade into the jars and screwing on the lids, you'll find the lids are sucked in tightly by the cooling jars.

SIMPLE JAM RECIPE

900g fruit (blackberries, plums, raspberries or strawberries), prepared weight
 900g golden granulated sugar
 Knob of butter

4 jam jars

Put the fruit into a preserving pan or large heavy-based saucepan. For blackberries, add 50ml of water and 1½ tbsp of lemon juice; for plums (halved and stoned), use 150ml of water; for strawberries, add 3 tbsp of lemon juice (no water); and for raspberries, add nothing. Bring to the boil.

Lower the heat. For blackberries, simmer for 15 minutes; for plums, simmer for 30-40 minutes; for raspberries, simmer for 2 minutes; for strawberries, simmer for 5 minutes. The fruit should be soft.

Tip in the sugar, stir over a very low heat until the sugar has completely dissolved. Raise the heat, bring to a full rolling boil, then rapidly boil blackberries for 10-12 minutes, plums for 10 minutes, raspberries for 5 minutes or strawberries for 20-25 minutes - don't stir though - until the setting point of 105C is reached.

Remove from the heat; skim off any excess scum, then stir a knob of butter across the surface (this helps to dissolve any remaining scum). Leave for about 15 mins so the fruit can settle. Pour into sterilised jars, label and seal.

Tip: Heat the jars (without lids) in the oven at 120°C, during the jam making. This helps sterilise. After adding the jam and sealing,

SIMPLE MARMALADE RECIPE

6-8 small oranges, weighing about 550g

Juice of 1 lemon

1.4 litres water

1.1 kg granulated sugar

Slice the oranges in half. Using a metal spoon, scoop out the flesh over a bowl to collect any juice, leaving the pith behind. Reserve the shells.

Put the flesh, juice and pips in a food processor and blend until smooth. Push the purée through a sieve into a preserving pan or large heavy-based saucepan. Now scoop out as much of the pith from the shells as possible. Slice the rind into very thin matchstick strips and add these to the sieved flesh in the pan. Pour in the lemon juice and water. Bring to the boil.

Reduce the heat and simmer for 1 to 1 1/2 hours until the rind is very soft and the mixture has reduced by half.

Over a low heat, add the sugar and stir until it has dissolved. Boil for about 10 minutes, skimming off any froth on the surface.

Spoon a little of the marmalade onto a cold plate and place in the fridge. If it sets to a jelly the marmalade is cooked. If necessary, cook for a further 5-10 minutes and test again. Allow the marmalade to cool slightly and then pour into sterilized jars.

Children, parents and staff enjoy watching Lemurs on a school trip to the Yorkshire Wildlife Park.

GRAPEFRUIT MARMALADE (from Mount Pleasant Garage, Grindleford)

1 Grapefruit
1 Lemon
1 Orange
400g Sugar
500mls of "liquid"

Grate rind from fruit and place in fridge. Put peeled fruit in large pan, cover with water and boil until soft. Cover pan and leave overnight. Take fruit out and squeeze into another pan. Add grated fruit rind. Add 500mls of the liquid from the first pan (topped up if needs be) and boil for one hour. Add the sugar (400g per 500mls of liquid) and boil rapidly for 15mins. Test a few drops on a saucer – if it crinkles when touched it's ready. Otherwise boil for a little longer. Leave to cool a little then place in warmed jars and seal.

PUDDINGS

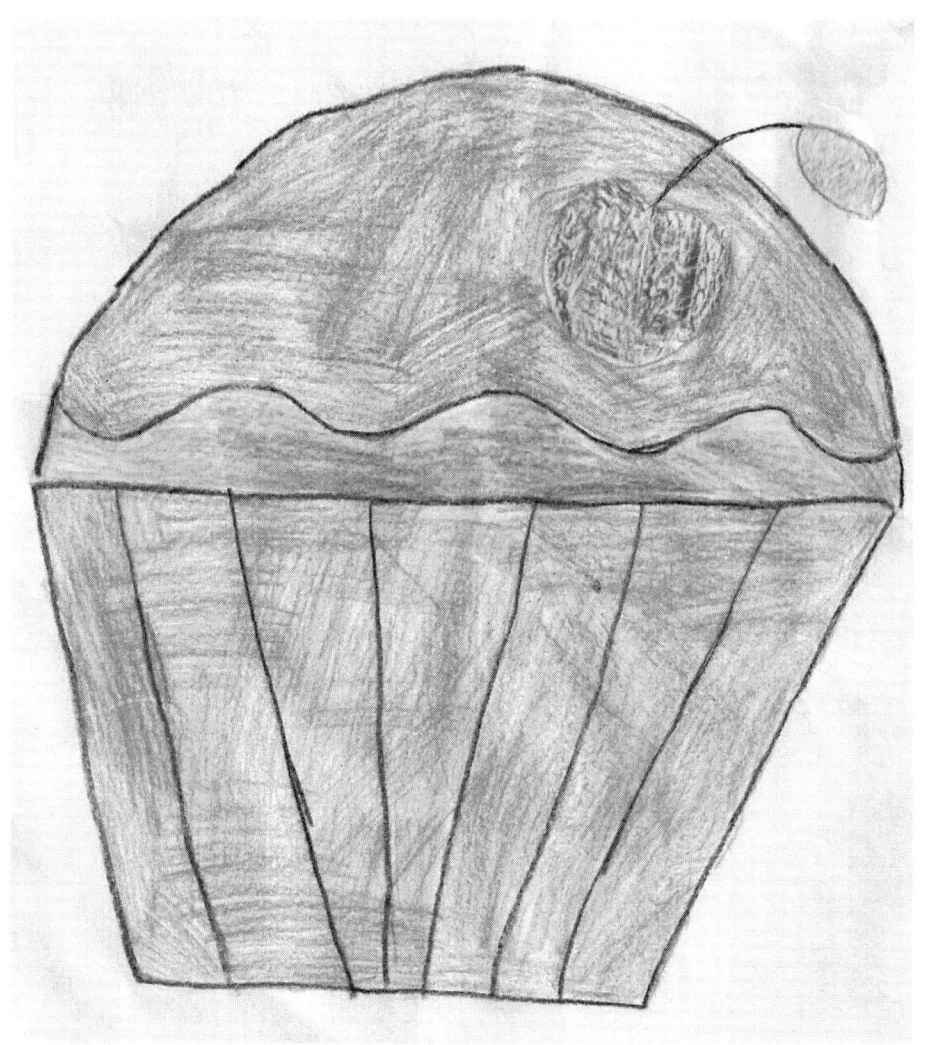

Illustration by Hazel Platts

CAKES AND BUNS

SPONGE CAKE (By Bryn Heason)

100g Self-raising flour
100g Butter
100g Caster sugar
2 Eggs
Rind of one lemon
Jam

Grease two sandwich tins and line with greaseproof paper. Cream butter and sugar until fluffy. Beat eggs in a basin and add to cream mix. Fold in flour and lemon rind. Divide into 2 tins. Bake at 190°C for 20-25mins. When cool sandwich with Jam in between and sprinkle with caster sugar.

LEMON DRIZZLE CAKE (by Holly Thornton)

For the Cake Mixture:
200g soft unsalted butter
250g caster sugar
3 eggs
Lemon zest
250g self-raising flour
½ teaspoon baking powder

100ml milk.

For the topping:
100g caster sugar
Lemon juice
Lemon zest

Grease the baking tin and line with greaseproof paper.
Preheat the oven to 180°C/Gas Mark 4. Put the soft butter,
sugar, eggs and lemon zest into a large mixing bowl. Sift the
flour and baking powder into the bowl and then pour in the
milk. Beat with a wooden spoon or an electric whisk until the
ingredients are completely smooth. Transfer the mixture to
the prepared tin and bake until the cake is a good golden
brown and firm and a cocktail stick inserted into the centre
comes out clean – 50 to 60 minutes.

Meanwhile, make the topping. Mix the sugar with the lemon
juice and zest to make a runny glaze. As soon as the cake is
cooked, remove it from the oven and stand the tin on a wire
cooling rack. Prick the top of the cake all over with a cocktail
stick and then quickly spoon the lemon topping over so that it
trickles down into the holes. Leave to cool completely before
removing the cake from the tin and discarding the lining
paper. Serve cut into thick slices.

YUMMY QUADRUPLE CHOCOLATE CAKE (The Barnett family)

200g plain flour
1/2 teaspoon bicarbonate of soda
50g cocoa
275g caster sugar
175g soft unsalted butter
2 eggs
1 tablespoon vanilla essence
80ml natural yoghurt
125ml boiling water
175g dark chocolate

For syrup
1 teaspoon cocoa
125mls water
100g caster sugar
25g dark chocolate

Pre-heat oven to gas mark 3and line 900g baking tin with greaseproof paper.
Put flour, bicarbonate of soda, cocoa, sugar, eggs, vanilla essence, yoghurt into food processor and blitz! Pour in boiling water and the dark chocolate (in chips). Save some chocolate for grating later! Place into the tin and cook for 1 hour. 15 minutes before end put syrup ingredients into pan and boil for 5 minutes (until they form a syrup). Take cake out and cool. Pour on syrup and then sprinkle with grated chocolate

Chocolate Cake

Quick and special

Ingredients:-

    6 oz plain flour

    1 level teaspoon bi-carbonate soda

    1 round teaspoon baking powder.

    2 level tablespoons of cocoa

    2 " " of golden syrup.

    5oz. caster sugar.

    2 eggs

$\frac{1}{4}$ pint milk + $\frac{1}{4}$ pint oil to make $\frac{1}{2}$ pint.

In a large mixing bowl sift flour, bi-carbonate soda, baking powder and cocoa. Make well in centre. Drop in caster sugar, golden syrup and 2 eggs. Pour in oil and milk mixture.

Beat until smooth, (I use a mixer) then divide between 2 x 8" dia. tins.

Cook 30 mins in a preheated oven Gas no. 3 or 325 F. Cool. Then fill and top with chocolate icing and decorate as desired.

The recipe is ideal to make a Black Forest gateau.

Wendy Cook.

Recipe from the Old Cookbook by Wendy Cook (former teacher at Grindleford Primary School)

PLATTS FAMILY CHOCOLATE BIRTHDAY CAKE RECIPE
(by Hazel Platts)

4oz self-raising flour
1tsp baking powder
4oz caster sugar
4oz soft margarine/butter
2 large or 3 small eggs

1oz cocoa powder
1 tsp instant coffee powder
3 teaspoons very hot water

For the icing:

4oz icing sugar
1oz cocoa powder
2oz butter
3 teaspoons water
3oz sugar

For a large cake, triple the quantities and divide the mixture between two same size tins to bake.

For the cake, preheat oven to 180°C and mix together the self raising flour, baking powder, caster sugar, butter and the eggs. Then mix together the cocoa powder, instant coffee powder & hot water and add this to the first mixture. Pour into a greased, lined 8" cake tin and bake until a skewer inserted into the cake comes out clean. Begin checking after 20 to 25 minutes, depending on the quantity of mixture. Leave to cool.

For the icing, sift into a bowl the icing sugar and the cocoa powder. Into a saucepan put the butter, water and sugar and bring to the boil. Boil for one minute and then add the icing sugar and the cocoa powder. Leave the delicious, chocolaty mass to cool before icing the cake (There is enough icing to add an inside layer as well as covering the top and sides). If necessary, add a little more icing sugar to get the right consistency. Decorate the cake if you wish.

CHAMBERS FAMILY BOILED FRUITCAKE (by Jo Burn)

My Nannie always had this cake in her cupboard, and it's a recipe that's stood the test of time for the whole family. It's so easy to make, stays moist and keeps well.

4oz butter

6oz granulated sugar

14oz good quality mixed fruit

8 fl oz water

1 level teaspoon bicarbonate of soda

1 heaped teaspoon of mixed spice

2 beaten eggs

4 oz plain flour

4 oz self-raising flour

Pinch of salt

Preheat oven to 180°C / gas mark 4.

Line a 7 inch square / 8 inch round tin.

Place butter, sugar, fruit, water, bicarb and mixed spice in a pan and bring to the boil. Simmer for 1 minute. Allow to cool.

Add eggs, flour and salt to the mixture. Mix well. Pour into tin.

Bake for 75 minutes.

ORLY'S PINK CHOCOLATE BUNS (by Orly Seligman)

For the cake:
100g plain flower
20g cocoa powder
140g caster sugar
1.5tsp baking powder
Pinch of salt
40g unsalted butter at room temperature
120ml whole milk
1 egg
$\frac{1}{4}$tsp of vanilla extract
12 cupcake cases

For the icing:

100g white chocolate
2 tablespoons milk
140g (5 oz) unsalted butter, softened
275g icing sugar
1 teaspoon of vanilla
1 teaspoon pink food colouring (enough to mix to desired depth of colour)

To decorate:
Pink sugar sprinkles
Hearts cut out of roll-able fondant etc

Preheat the oven to 170°C (325°F) gas 3. Put flour, cocoa, sugar and baking powder, salt and butter in a mixer or use electric whisk. Mix together until you have a sandy consistency. Whisk milk, egg and vanilla in a jug. Slowly pour half into the mixture, beat to combine and then turn the mixer up to high speed to get rid of any lumps.

Turn the mixer down to a slower speed and pour in the remaining mixture. Continue to mix for a couple of minutes. Do not over-mix. Spoon mixture into the 12 cases and cook for 20 minutes.

To make the butter cream:
Break up the white chocolate and milk into a heat proof bowl and melt over a pan of boiling water. Stir well and set aside. Place the butter, icing sugar, vanilla extract and melted chocolate in the bowl of a food processor. Blend until it

comes together. Spoon into a piping bag and decorate cooled cupcakes. Let the kids sprinkle on the pink sugar and decorate with fondant hearts. Use a piping bag and metal nozzle to pipe onto top of cooled cupcakes.
Eat. (Yum)

> Why I Like Grindleford Primary School.......
> "It's really cool and we have really cool teachers!"
> Ruby

CHRISTMAS PUDDING (from the Maynard Arms Grindleford)

At the end of Christmas term each year The Maynard Arms staff invite the Grindleford Primary School children to their kitchens. There they are shown how to make their own Christmas Puddings, using the Maynard Arms special recipe below.

225g/8oz soft light brown sugar
225g/8oz vegetarian suet
340g/12oz sultanas
340g/12oz raisins
225g/8oz cherries
110g/4oz candied peel, chopped
110g/4oz plain flour

110g/4oz fresh white breadcrumbs
55g/2oz flaked almonds
5 eggs, beaten
1 Level tsp ground cinnamon
1 level tsp mixed spice
5g/1 level tsp freshly grated nutmeg
pinch of salt

100ml/10fl oz stout
50ml/5fl oz rum

Lightly grease 4x600ml/1 pint or 2x1.2 litre/2 pint pudding basins. Mix together all the dry ingredients. Stir in the eggs, stout and rum and mix well. Spoon the mix into basins. Put a circle of baking parchment and foil over the top of each basin and tie securely with string. Make a string handle from one side of the basin to the other so it is easier to pick the basin out of the pan after cooking. Put the basins in a large steamer of boiling water and cover with a lid. Boil for 5-6 hours, topping the boiling water up from time to time, if necessary. If you do not have a steamer, put the basins in a large pan on inverted saucers on the base. Pour in boiling water to come a third of the way up the sides of the pudding bowls. Cover and steam as before.

MAYA'S MAGNIFICENT FLOURLESS CHOCOLATE FUDGE CAKE (by Maya Seligman)

(With many thanks to Mr Ottolenghi for lending us the recipe)
Serves 8

240g unsalted butter cut into small cubes
265g dark chocolate (52% cocoa solids) cut into small pieces
95 g dark chocolate (70% cocoa solids) cut into small pieces
290 g light muscovado sugar
4 tablespoons water
5 large free range eggs separated
1 pinch salt
Cocoa powder for dusting

Preheat the oven to 170°C. Grease a 20cm springform cake tin and line the base and sides with baking parchment. Place the butter and both types of chocolate in a large heatproof bowl

Put the brown sugar and water in a small saucepan and stir to mix and then bring to the boil over a medium heat. Pour the boiling syrup over the butter and chocolate and stir well until they have melted and you are left with a runny chocolate sauce

Stir in the egg yolks one at a time and set aside until mixture cools. Put the egg whites and salt in a large bowl and whisk to a firm, but not too dry meringue. Using a rubber spatula or large metal spoon, gently fold the meringue into the cooled chocolate mixture, a third at a time. The whites should be fully incorporated but there is no harm if you can see small bits of meringue in the mix.

Pour 800 grams (about $\frac{2}{3}$ of the mixture) into the prepared cake tin and level gently with a palette knife. Leave the rest of the batter for later – place the cake in the oven and bake for about 40 minutes until a skewer inserted in the centre comes out almost clean.

Remove from the oven and leave to cool completely. Flatten the top of the cake with a palette knife. Don't worry about breaking the crust – pour the rest of the batter on the top and level the surface again.
Return to the oven and bake for 20 - 25 mins. The cake should still have moist crumbs when checked with the skewer. Leave to cool completely before removing from the tin. Dust with cocoa powder and serve

The cake will keep covered at room temperature for 4 days if you can leave it that long…. It is YUMMY, on its own, or with raspberries and cream.

DERWENT GALLERY SUMMER CUPCAKES

3 eggs
Butter
Sugar
Self-raising flour
Desiccated coconut (3 handfuls)
Raspberries (3 handfuls)

Break 3 eggs into a bowl and weigh them.
Add the same amount of soft butter, sugar and flour.
Beat ingredients together.
Into the batter add three handfuls of desiccated coconut
and three handfuls of washed raspberries.
Fold gently into the mixture.
Spoon into cupcake cases or tins
Cook at 180°C for 15 – 20mins

PROFITEROLES (By Benny Crowson)

140g butter, softened
200g self-raising flour
1.5 tsp baking powder
200g golden caster sugar
3 large eggs
6 tbsp milk
Finely grated zest 1 large orange.

To finish
3 tbsp orange juice.
50g golden caster sugar.
50g dark chocolate.

Cooking Instructions: Heat oven to 180°C/fan 160°C/gas 4. Butter and line the base of a 1.2-litre loaf tin. Put all the cake ingredients into a bowl and beat with a hand whisk or wooden spoon for 3-5 mins, until light and fluffy. Spoon the mix into the tin and level the top.
Bake for 40-50 mins, until golden brown and firm to the touch. Meanwhile, heat the orange juice and sugar gently in a small pan, stirring until dissolved. When the cake is cooked, remove it from the oven and spoon over the orange mix. Leave to cool in the tin, then remove and cool completely on a wire rack.
Break up the chocolate and melt over a pan of simmering water or in the microwave on Medium for 1-2 mins. Drizzle over the cake and leave to set

RASPBERRY PASTRY SWIRLS (by Tom B)

To make about 40 swirls you will need:
225g ready-made puff pastry cut from a block and taken out of the fridge 20 mins before you start.
Icing sugar, for dusting
3 tablespoons of raspberry jam
1 tablespoon of caster sugar

Lay two baking trays on baking parchment and draw around them. Cut out the shapes, then lay them in the trays. Dust icing sugar onto a clean surface and a rolling pin. Then, roll out the pastry to a square as wide as the rolling pin. Trim the edges of the pastry, so that they are straight. Then, cut pastry down middle to make two rectangles.
Spread half of the jam over each piece of pastry. Leave a thin border around the edges of each piece. Brush water along one edge of one piece, then roll the pastry from opposite edge. Repeat this with the other piece. Wrap the rolls in clingfilm, then chill in a fridge for 30 minutes. Set oven to 180°C. Unwrap the rolls, and cut into 1cm slices. Put the slices onto the baking trays and space them out. Sprinkle half of the sugar on the swirls. Bake them. for 10-12 minutes, until they are golden. Lift out of oven and sprinkle

sugar over the swirls. After 5 minutes, move onto a wire rack and leave to cool.

BAKED EGG & NUTMEG TART,BLUEBERRY COMPOTE (from The White Lion, Great Longstone)

<u>For the Compote</u>

Handful of Blueberries (frozen)
Desert spoon of sugar

Heat the blueberries in a pan until warm and completely thawed. Add sugar and stir until dissolved. Allow to cool.

<u>For the Sweet Pastry</u>

2 eggs
100g sugar
250g butter
400g plain flour
Pinch of salt
12 inch round tin

Cream together the eggs and sugar. Add the softened butter and continue to mix for a few seconds. Add the flour and salt. Mix very gently until smooth. Place in the fridge for half an hour before baking blind (do not pierce the base)

For the Egg Custard Filling

375ml milk
375ml double cream
200g sugar
2 vanilla pods
5 eggs
Grated nutmeg

Warm the milk and double cream together. In a separate bowl mix together the eggs, the seeds from the vanilla pods and the sugar. Slowly add the warmed milk and cream to the egg mixture, continually whisk as you go. Pour the combined mixture into the pastry case and sprinkle with nutmeg. Bake at 170 C for 20-30 minutes or until set.

TRAY BAKING
(More traybakes in chapter "Grindleford Gallop")

MALTESER TRAYBAKE (from Calver Sough Nurseries)

100g butter
200g milk chocolate
3 tablespoons Golden Syrup
225g Digestive biscuits (finely crushed)
225g Maltesers

Melt together the butter, chocolate and syrup – then add the crushed biscuits and the Maltesers. Mix together and pour into a lined baking tin and place into the fridge until set.
Tip: Pour some melted white chocolate onto the top for an extra special traybake!

DATE TRAYBAKE WITH FUDGE TOPPING (by Mary Wren)

350g chopped dates
1½ teaspoon bicarbonate of soda
350g soft brown sugar
125g melted butter
2 small beaten eggs
1½ teaspoon vanilla essence
425g plain flour
1½ teaspoon baking powder
85g chopped walnuts (optional)

Topping
85g soft brown sugar
40g melted butter
3 tablespoons cream or evaporated milk

Line a 30cm x 20cm baking tray with baking parchment. Cover dates and bicarbonate of soda with 1½ cups (325mls) boiling water and leave to cool.

Sieve flour and baking powder together and add all ingredients to the date mixture and mix well

Pour into tin and bake at 180°C for 40mins until firm to the touch. Leave to cool

To make topping put all ingredients into a saucepan and, stirring all the time, boil for 3mins. Continue to stir and allow to cool slightly until it begins to thicken and spread over the cake. Cut into pieces.

CHOCOLATE BROWNIES (By Leela)

175g Butter
175g Light Moscavado sugar
175g Plain chocolate
2 large eggs
225g Self-raising Flour

Preheat oven to 180°C. Line a 25cm by 25cm baking tray with greaseproof paper. Place chocolate and butter into a heat resistant bowl over hot water. Add the sugar to the melted mixture then cool. Beat the eggs and add to cooled mixture, then fold in the flour. Spread the mixture into the tray, bake for 15-20mins until firm. Allow to cool then cut into squares and cool on a rack.

MARCIA'S FAVOURITE FRUIT, OAT AND SEEDS BARS (by Marcia Platts)

140g light muscovado sugar
3 tbsp golden syrup
140g butter
250g rolled oats
85g raisins or sultanas
85g walnut pieces (or use your favourite nuts, roughly chopped)
50g sesame or mixed seeds
25g dried cranberries
50g ready to eat apricots, finely chopped.
Heat the oven to 160°C (fan 140°C). Gently heat the sugar, golden syrup and butter in a pan until the sugar and butter have both melted. Stir in the oats, raisins, walnuts, seeds and cranberries into the pan until coated in the butter.

Spoon half the oaty mix into a traybake tin (23cm x 23cm or thereabouts!!). Scatter the apricots over the top and then top with the remaining oat mix. Pack the mix down well and smooth with the back of a metal spoon. Bake for 35 minutes or until dark golden. Leave to cool completely before cutting into 16 bars with a sharp knife.

FLAPJACK (by Emily Mottershaw)
100g butter or margarine
50g demerara sugar
30ml golden syrup
125g porridge oats
25g plain flour
Melt butter, sugar and syrup over a low heat, stirring until dissolved. Remove from heat. Mix in porridge oats and flour. Press into a well greased 20.5cm shallow square tin. Bake for 15-20 minutes at 180°C, gas mark 4 until golden brown. Mark into bars. Leave to cool before removing from tin.

BAKEWELL SLICE (from Cotswold Outdoor, Bakewell)

At 3.30pm, just when we are at our hungriest, customers arrive in the shop with brown paper bags bulging with puddings and tarts – we thought we'd share this recipe with you.

For the sweet pastry:
350g/12oz plain flour
pinch of salt
125g/4½oz chilled unsalted butter
125g/4½oz caster sugar

2 free-range eggs, whole and 1 egg, yolk only

For the filling:
150g butter
150g ground almonds
150g caster sugar
4 eggs
325g raspberry jam
100g flaked almonds

Start with the pastry:
Preheat the oven to 180°C. Grease and flour a 25 x 30cm tin.
Stir the flour and salt together in a large mixing bowl. Take
the butter from the fridge, cut into chunks and add the
butter to the flour. Rub in the mixture until it looks like big
crumbs. Add the sugar, mix together the eggs and egg yolk,
and add to the mixture. Mix until the dough comes together
in a ball. Lightly flour a work surface, tip the pastry ball out
onto it. Knead to a smooth soft dough and shape the pastry
into a square to fit into the tin. Press the pastry into the
corners and edges of the tin. Spread raspberry jam all over
the bottom.

Now the filling:

Tip the almonds into a frying pan (without any oil or butter) and gently heat them. Keep stirring them so they don't burn. They should go a golden brown colour. Melt the butter and set aside. Whisk the almonds, sugar and eggs in a separate mixing bowl. Add the melted butter to the almond mix gradually, mixing as you go. Pour the mixture over the jam making sure you cover the entire jammy base. Sprinkle the toasted almonds on the top, then place in the oven for about 30-35 minutes until it is golden brown. Let it cool before removing from the tray and cutting. Enjoy!

CORN FLAKE TART (by Joe Luscombe)

For the Pastry:
250g plain flour
125g butter or margarine
Cold water
Red jam

For the Cornflake topping:
125g caster sugar
125g butter
220g cornflakes
125g golden syrup

Pre heat oven to 200°C/Gas Mark 6. Place flour and fat into a large bowl and rub in the fat until the mixture resembles breadcrumbs. Add a dessert spoon of water until you form a ball. Roll out the pastry, line a tin 30cm by 12cm and bake for 15 minutes. Allow to cool then spread with jam. Turn the oven down to 170°C/Gas Mark 4. Place the sugar, syrup and butter in a large pan and heat gently until the butter has melted. then add cornflakes slowly. Mix well to make sure each cornflake is sticky. Place the cornflake mix into the jammy tart case and press down well. Bake in the oven for 10 minutes. When cold cut into squares.

CARAMEL SHORTBREAD (by Archie & Bertie McMullan)
"Hide it from everyone!"

225g Plain flour

75g Caster sugar

375g Unsalted butter

379g can sweetened condensed milk

4 Tablespoons Golden Syrup

325g Plain chocolate

8 by 8 inch square brownie tin or similar, greased and the bottom lined with waxed paper

Preheat the oven to 170°C / Gas Mark 3

Put the flour and sugar into a bowl and rub in 175g of butter, clumping the dough together to make a ball. Press this sandy shortbread mixture into the tin and smooth it down. Prick with a fork and cook for five minutes, then lower the oven to 150°C / gas mark 2, and cook for a further 30-40 minutes until pale golden and no longer doughy. Let it cool in the tin. Melt the remaining 200g of butter in a large microwavable bowl, then add condensed milk and golden syrup. Heat in the microwave until the butter is melted. Then whisk together. Heat for 1 minute at a time. Whisk after each minute. This may take up to 6 minutes until boiling – it's ready when it's thickened and turned a light golden brown. Pour this molten toffee over the shortbread and leave to set. Melt chocolate and pour over the fudge mixture and leave to cool. Once set, cut the caramel shortbread into pieces. Hide it from everybody!

Makes about 24 pieces.

ROCKY ROADS (By Lauren Fletcher)

125g Soft butter
300g Dark chocolate (broken into pieces)
3 tbsp Golden Syrup
200g Rich Tea biscuits
100g mini marshmallows
2 tbsp icing sugar for dusting

Melt the butter chocolate and golden syrup in a saucepan.

Take out about 125mls of the mixture and set aside.

Break up the biscuits in a bag.

Fold the biscuits into the chocolate mixture, then add the marshmallows.

Place mixture in a foil tray and pour the mixture set aside (above) on top. Smooth it all over!

Place in fridge for 2 hours. Dust with icing sugar and cut into 24 pieces.

SMILE Village Hall Cake (from Stoney Middleton Interest & Leisure Enterprise)

We're ready to take the next step and put up the village hall changing rooms & showers on the playing field. So here's the recipe! Form a level base of concrete and leave to dry and harden. Form the pre-fabricated panels of Cornish wood into a village hall shape on the concrete base. Layer the Welsh slate on top of the building. Coat the sides with local limestone for authentic local flavour!

JAM PIN WHEELS (By Fay Bowman)

320g ready rolled puff pastry
jam or the filling of your choice
milk to brush over the pastry.

Roll out the pastry, cover with jam filling spread thinly, roll it up so it looks like a swiss roll. Cut into 8 pieces, put the rings onto a baking sheet. Brush the milk over the top of them. Place them in the oven Gas 7 or 220 electric for 30mins or until golden brown.

Rosalie Biscuits.

Makes <u>lots</u> of big cookies!

1 lb plain flour
1 level tablespoon baking powder
1 teaspoon bicarb.
10 oz marg. or butter
10 oz sugar
1 good ~~tab~~ lespoon syrup.

1. Sieve together flour, baking powder, bicarb.
2. Rub in butter/marg.
3. Add sugar + syrup (warm + runny is best!).
4. Mix well - (add extra flavouring now).
5. When like dough, roll golf-ball sized pieces of mixture, flatten slightly with a fork onto a baking sheet.
   Bake 15 mins, Gas 4, 350°F. 180°

Delicious with a ~~generous~~ handful of choc chips, or chopped stem ginger, or fruit, added at the mixing stage!

~~from~~
Sally Turnbull.

Recipe from the Old Cookbook by Sally Turnbull and supplied by Sally and OUTSIDE Ltd, Hathersage.

PANCAKES GALORE!

PANCAKES (by Anna Poulson)

Half a pint of milk
Pinch salt
One egg
125g Plain flour
Butter

Get a bowl and crack the egg into it. Whisk it up. Add flour milk and pinch of salt and whisk until smooth.

Put the pan on the stove and put a bit of butter in (so the mixture won't stick). Wait until it's steaming then get a scoop of the mixture and put it in. Wait for a couple of minutes and use a spatula to flip it over. Look underneath the pancake to see if it's ready then put it on the plate.
And that is how you make a pancake!

PERFECT PANCAKES (by Daniel Harby)

Can be a pudding or for camping!
1 mug of plain flour
1 mug of milk
1 egg
(use the same mug)

Put all the ingredients in a bowl and mix to a thick, creamy batter. Drop 2 to 3 tablespoons of batter into a hot, greased pancake / frying pan. Cook for 2 to 3 minutes on each side until bubbles begin to appear. Serve with sugar, lemon, ice cream, jam, chocolate spread, or fill with ham and cheese and bake in the oven. Fruit – e.g. blueberries and banana can be added for breakfast pancakes.

> *Why I Like Grindleford Primary School.......*
> *"Because it's very fun and they make the lessons very fun"*
> *Ezri Petts*

OSCAR'S SUPER PANCAKES (by Oscar Codd)

Oscar

110g plain flour
Pinch salt
2 Eggs
200mls milk mixed with 75mls water
2 tablespoons melted butter

Sift flour and place in blender with all the other ingredients. Blend until smooth. Heat frying pan with a little butter. Add enough mixture to swill around and cover base of pan. Cook for around 30seconds each side. Serve with lemon juice and sugar or anything else delicious you like. Oscar's Tip – Especially nice with Lemon Curd!

BANANA PANCAKES (By Ellie Detchen)
100g Self-raising Flour
1 free range egg
175mls milk
40g self raising wholemeal flour
2 tablespoons caster sugar
2 peeled bananas
Butter for frying

Put the flour, milk and sugar in a bowl and stir. Add beaten egg and mix well. Mash bananas in a separate bowl. Put butter in frying pan and roll it around the pan. Cook for 2 minutes

CHICKEN PANCAKES (from Eric Boocock at Eyam Hall Buttery)
Hopefully makes 4

This is a Monday teatime meal made almost entirely of leftovers from Sunday lunch. The kids will love it, and the recipe might just help get rid of your Monday Blues!

Provided you haven't had the family on starvation rations for the last 10 days or so, you'll need:

Whatever bits of chicken meat the kids can salvage from the pile of skin and bones lying drearily on a greasy cracked plate in the middle of the table. There's bound to be about 120gms if they're good at this;

About the same amount of untouched peas, carrots and green beans that you could neither bribe nor force the family to consume;

Add a small onion if the purse strings can stretch that far. Oh, and a chicken stock cube wouldn't go amiss either;

600mls or 1pt of left over Yorkshire pudding mixture (If you've got that much left over when you're only cooking for 4, then I'm glad you don't work in my kitchen).

Take the onion and remove skin (from the onion, not from your fingers), and roughly chop. If the cat hasn't jumped onto the kitchen table whilst you've been messing around with the onion, you should still have the pile of chicken meat, so slam that into the pan with the onions.

Take the veg and tip the lot into the pan with the other rubbish, crumble the stock cube over the disgusting looking mess and just cover with cold water. (I meant cover the chicken mixture, not yourself, you great dumpling!).

Once you've towelled yourself dry and returned from the hairdresser's, bring the chicken mixture to the boil and simmer gently for 5 minutes. Gradually pour in some of the Yorkshire pudding mixture until the chicken and other bits and pieces start to boil and thicken.

Make 4 pancakes with the rest of the Yorkshire Pudding mixture, taking care not to stick the pancakes to the ceiling or hitting the cat on the head with the hot pan.

Fill each pancake with chicken mixture and serve with anything you want. The kids won't care, hubby won't even notice and the cat will have moved house by the time you all sit down at the table!

Enjoy

Spinach & Walnut Pancakes

you need
1 pt Milk
1/4 pt Single cream
1/2 pt. Cider
Cornflour or thickener
garlic purée
teaspoon curry
pkt. frozen Spinach
1/2 lb walnut Halves.

6 oz. cheddar cheese

Basic pancake mix
for 6 pancakes.

Boil up the milk add the cream, cider, thickener garlic and curry, beating all the time, with a good fork full of thickener it Should be a runny custard consistency.

Put a pancake into each of the Six soup bowls drop at least 4 walnut halves and two tablespoons of Spinach — fold the pancake round these then turn upside down pour over the Sauce until the pancake is covered — generously grate the cheese on the top — put in the oven until the top is nice and brown.

Serve on its own or with Salad or chips.

Sally Fletcher

Recipe from the Old Cookbook by Barbara Sally Fletcher (Sally's children Annabelle and Peta were former pupils at Grindleford Primary School)

SCONES

GRACIE'S SUPER SCONES. (By Grace Marshall)

8oz self raising flour
2oz butter
1oz caster sugar
2 oz currants
1 egg
¼ pint of milk

Preheat oven to 200°C. Rub the butter into the flour to create bread crumbs. Add sugar and currants. Bind mixture together with the egg and milk. Roll out into 1.5cm slab and cut into round shapes.
Bake in oven for 12 mins. Hey presto Gracie's super scones are ready to eat! Yum Yum!

MINI WHEAT-FREE CHEESE SCONES (By Amelia Paraskevie Clark)

80g medium cheddar cheese
175g gluten free self raising flour
$\frac{1}{2}$ level tsp baking powder
A pinch of salt
25g butter
100ml milk
Milk for glazing
4cm round and heart shaped cutters
2 greased baking trays

Preheat the oven to 220°C, gas mark 7.

Grate the cheese then sift the flour, baking powder and salt into a bowl. Cut the butter into small pieces and add to the bowl. Rub into the flour until the mixture resembles fine breadcrumbs. Add 40g of the cheddar and mix in well. Add the milk and using a blunt knife, mix everything together to form soft dough. Place on a floured surface and roll out to 1cm thick. Then use the cutters to cut out circles and hearts. Place the scones on the baking tray spacing apart. Brush with milk and sprinkle with a little grated cheese on each one. Bake for about 8 minutes until risen and golden. Cool on a wire rack. Eat while warm with butter.

BISCUITS & MORE

ANZAC BISCUITS (by Toby Marshall)

Toby was born in New Zealand so here's a "Kiwi" recipe that makes 20 lovely biscuits!

$\frac{1}{2}$ cup plain flour

$\frac{1}{3}$ cup sugar

$\frac{2}{3}$ cup coconut

$\frac{3}{4}$ cup rolled oats

1 tablespoon of syrup

$\frac{1}{2}$ teaspoon baking powder

2 tablespoon boiling water

Mix flour sugar coconut and rolled oats. Melt butter and syrup in a pan. Dissolve baking soda into boiling water and add to butter and syrup. Add mixture to the dry ingredients. Add level tablespoon of mixture onto cold greased trays (they grow when cooked!). Bake at 180°C for 15mins or until golden.

QUICK YUMMY CHEESECAKES (By Eleanor Ives)
Serves 4

4 Digestive biscuits
100g Cream Cheese

2 tbsp icing sugar

125ml double cream

1 tbsp lemon juice

½ tsp vanilla extract

Approximately 8 strawberries (my favourite) or your favourite fruit in small pieces

4 small ramekins/glasses(150ml capacity).

Take the cream cheese out of the fridge to bring to room temperature. Put the biscuits in a freezer type bag and crush with a rolling pin until they are crumbs. Put the cream cheese and icing sugar in a bowl and whisk by hand. Add the cream, lemon juice and vanilla and whisk gently to combine. Divide the biscuit crumbs equally between the 4 glasses and gently smooth. Spoon the cream cheese mixture on top of each one covering the biscuit base. Top with small pieces of fruit.

NAN'S CUSTARD (Crème brûlée)

Makes 7 servings

10 fl.oz (300ml) double cream

10 fl.oz. full cream milk

½ vanilla pod, cut open to release the seeds

5 egg yolks, size 2

3 oz (75g) caster sugar

½ teaspoon natural vanilla essence

7 heaped teaspoons Demerara sugar (for the brûlée topping.)

Preheat oven to 150°C. Place the cream, milk and vanilla pod in a pan. Heat gently, until near boiling point. Lightly beat the egg yolks, caster sugar and vanilla essence together in a bowl. Gradually pour the hot liquid onto the egg yolks, stirring as you do so. When well-mixed, pour through a fine sieve into another bowl.

Sit seven 150ml ramekins in a baking tray which will hold enough water to come half-way up the sides of the ramekins. Stir the custard gently so that any foam will be incorporated into it. Any that is not, spoon off. Then, divide the mixture between the ramekins. Place the tray of ramekins on the front of the middle shelf of the pre-heated oven. Pour enough boiling water into the tray to come half-way up the sides of the ramekins, and then gently slide the tray in. Bake for approximately 25 minutes until set.

Check after 20 minutes by pulling the tray out a little and gently shaking a ramekin. If the contents wobbles very slightly it is set. If it looks too soft, return it to the heat, and continue to cook until set. Remove from the oven and allow to cool in the water.

When cool, place on a tray and refrigerate. They must be cool before you place them in the fridge, otherwise water will condense onto their surface which will spoil what should be a crisp caramel topping.
At least 1½ hours and at most 4 hours before serving, pre-heat the grill to very hot. Spoon a teaspoonful of demerara

sugar onto each custard, place as many as will fit under the grill on a metal tray and grill until the sugar melts. Check constantly and remove immediately the sugar has caramelised to a golden brown.

Allow to cool for 5 minutes, and then return them to the refrigerator. Serve while still crisp. Note. Youngsters seem to prefer the un-brûléed custard.

Exploring the school pond at the after school Summer Picnic 2013

USING THE FRIDGE/FREEZER

BANANA & COCONUT ICE CREAM (The Heason Family)
Serves 6-8
85g Creamed Coconut (chopped)
600ml Double Cream
225g Icing Sugar
2 Bananas
1 tsp Lemon Juice

Why I Like Grindleford Primary School.......
"I've forgotten!"
Albie Wrench

Put the coconut in a small bowl. Add just enough boiling water to cover and stir until dissolved. Leave to cool.
Whip the cream with the icing sugar until thick but still floppy. Mash the bananas with the lemon juice and whisk gently into the cream together with the cold coconut. Transfer to a freezer proof container and freeze overnight. Serve in scoops with fresh fruit.

DADDY'S BROKEN BISUIT CAKE (By Elfie Burn)

6oz Butter
4oz Plain Chocolate
4 Tablespoons Golden Syrup
12oz Digestive Biscuits
4oz raisins (optional – can use other dried fruit also)
Large bar of milk chocolate

Smash up biscuits. Melt the butter in a pan, add half the chocolate and gently allow this to melt too. Mix the broken biscuits with dried fruit and add the melted ingredients, mixing well. Put in square cake tin and press down well. Place in fridge overnight. Melt remainder of chocolate to cover the top, leave to cool and set.

GRANDMA'S PEPPERMINT CREAMS (by Alice)

1 Egg white
350g White icing sugar & extra for shaping
3 Drops of peppermint essence
2 Drops of green food colouring
125g Dark chocolate broken into pieces

These tasty sweets are easy to make.
Whisk the egg until frothy. Sieve in the icing sugar and mix well. Add the peppermint essence and the colouring. Sprinkle icing sugar on to hands. Roll the mixture into balls. Flatten each one with a fork. Place in fridge for one hour until firm. Put the chocolate pieces in a heat proof bowl. Place bowl on a pan of water (about 5cm deep). When chocolate has melted

stir until smooth. Allow to cool a little. Dip each sweet into chocolate until half covered. Place them on a non-stick paper to set. Keep in a cool place or fridge until needed.

CHEAT'S TIRAMISU

400g soft cream cheese (eg Philadelphia)
Tin condensed milk
Packet of sponge fingers
½ pt black coffee (cold)
Tbsp brandy or similar (optional)
Cadburys Flake (or grated chocolate)

Cream together the cheese and condensed milk.

Mix coffee and brandy (if using). Pour coffee into shallow bowl and dip in a few sponge fingers at a time, turning after a few seconds, until they are soaked but not soggy. Put a single layer of sponge fingers into an oblong or oval serving dish then spread over half of the cream mixture. Repeat the two layers (the whole of the packet of sponge fingers may not be needed, depending on size of dish). Cover top with a flaked Flake or grated chocolate.

Cover and chill for a few hours or overnight.

Serves 6-8

Variation:

Use apple juice instead of coffee, and strawberries instead of flaked chocolate

CHEWY CHERRY CRUNCH (by Tom B)

To make about 50 squares you will need:

25g glace cherries

75g rice crispies

100g pink and white marshmallows

25g butter

An 18cm shallow square cake tin

1. Lay the tin on a piece of greaseproof paper. Draw around it, then cut out the square, just inside the line.

2. Using a paper towel, wipe cooking oil all over the inside of the tin. Press in the paper square and wipe oil over it, too.

3. Put the glace cherries onto a chopping board. Using a sharp knife, carefully cut them in half, then into small pieces.

4. Put the chopped cherries into a bowl, then add the rice crispies. Mix everything well with a wooden spoon.

5. Cut the marshmallows in half with a clean pair of scissors. Then, put the marshmallows and butter into a large saucepan.

6. Heat the mixture on a low heat, until everything has just melted. Stir it with a wooden spoon every now and then.
7. Take the pan off the heat, then add the cherry and rice crispy mixture. Stir it in. until all the pieces are covered.
8. Spoon the mixture into the tin and chill it in a fridge for 2 hours. Then, loosen the edges with a blunt knife.
9. Turn the crunch out onto a chopping board. Peel off the paper, then use a sharp knife to cut the crunch into squares.

CHOCOLATE BISCUIT CAKE (by William Hand)

40g-margarine or butter
30g-golden syrup
10g-cocoa powder
20g-raisins or sultanas
80g-sweet biscuits crushed chocolate

Melt the margarine in a saucepan add the raisins/sultanas syrup and cocoa powder. Then add the crushed biscuits. Once mixed together place in one tin. When cooled cover with a layer of chocolate.

BOB'S HEALTHY LOLLIPOPS (by Bob Stewart)

Bob Stewart has been the crossing patrol for Grindleford School children for 15 years. He knows all the children individually, and chats to all as they are safely guided across Grindleford's main road. A familiar face to all the children, Bob retires this year. We wish him a happy retirement!

Ingredients

1 mango
2 kiwis
1 peach
1 pear
Optional fruits for colour
  Raspberry
  Strawberry

Wash and peel all the fruits then cut into small pieces. Squeeze the pear to extract the juice. Blend the mango pieces (and, if using, the other fruits for colour) using the juice from the pear. Crush the kiwi and the peach. Scoop both purees into the ice lolly mould, layering them.

Place in freezer for minimum of four hours. That's it!

Tip: If you do not have ice lolly moulds, small yoghurt pots or even Ice Cube trays will do.

SMOOTHIE ICE LOLLIES (by Hazel and Marcia Platts)

You will need ice lolly moulds.

Fruit of choice eg strawberries, raspberries, blueberries etc.
Banana
Pear

or:

Smoothie juice ready made in a carton

Live natural yoghurt

extra treat: melted chocolate and sprinkles.

Throw the fruit into a blender (core and chop large fruits
such as the pear), add some big dollops of live natural yoghurt
and whizzzzzzzzzzzzzzzzzzzzz. Sieve to remove any seeds
OR
Grab a carton of smoothie juice.

Put a raspberry or two in the bottom of each ice lolly mould.
Add a few dollops of natural yoghurt and then add smoothie
juice up to the top of the mould. Put the tops on the moulds
and freeze for a couple of hours or overnight.

To finish, melt the chocolate, release the lollies from their
moulds by dipping the tray briefly in hot water. Dip each lolly
in the melted chocolate and then into the sugar sprinkles.
Serve immediately or keep in the freezer for about 1 week.

MARS BAR CAKE (from the 1st Curbar Guides)
This is a favourite of the Girl Guides! :-)

3 Mars Bars sliced
3 ozs of butter
3 to 4 ozs of Rice Krispies
1 block of cooking chocolate
2 x 7 inch sponge tins

Melt the butter and Mars bars together in a saucepan.
Take off the heat and add the Rice Krispies, stir until all of
the Rice Krispies are covered with the mixture.
Divide the mixture equally into two tins and press down flat
with spatula.
Melt chocolate and spread evenly on top of the cake mixture.
Place in the fridge until set.

MARION'S TIFFIN

4 ozs margarine
2 ozs sugar
1 tbsp drinking chocolate
1 tsp vanilla essence
1 packet Rich Tea biscuits, crushed (but not too small pieces)
4 ozs melted chocolate (plain)
1 large egg
4 ozs raisins

Melt margarine, sugar and drinking chocolate together, then add beaten egg, crushed biscuits, vanilla essence and raisins. Mix well and spread in a tray (11x8 ins or 200x280 cms), pressing down well. Cover with melted chocolate and leave to set.

Variations:
Use coconut instead of raisins
Use white or milk chocolate instead of plain

MORE PUDDINGS!

GROWN-UPS SUMMER JELLY (by Heather Jacques)
Serves 6
Takes 15mins to make, 10 mins to cook, plus chilling and 3
hours or overnight to set

A little oil for greasing
100g caster sugar
8 gelatine leaves
300ml Pimm's Squeeze of lemon juice and orange juice
150g strawberries, hulled & halved or quarters
100g cucumber, peeled, deseeded and cut into thin pieces
1 to 2 tbsp of very small fresh mint leaves
Extra fruit and cream to serve (optional)

Lightly grease a 1 litre jelly mould and set aside. Soak the
gelatine leaves in a bowl of cold water for 5 mins until
softened. Meanwhile, gently heat 300ml of water and the
sugar in a pan, stirring until dissolved. Bring to a gentle
simmer, then remove from the heat. Squeeze out as much
water as you can from the gelatine, then add to the hot sugar
syrup, stirring until dissolved. Cool slightly, then add the
Pimm's and the citrus juice. Once cool, arrange one third of

the strawberries, cucumber and mint in the mould and pour over just enough jelly to cover. Chill for 15 mins until just set. Add a second layer of the same and chill until set, then repeat once more. Chill for 3 hours or overnight. Serve with extra fruit and cream to taste.

THOMAS UNDER THE EIDERDOWN (This is a mystery recipe as we don't know who gave it to us!)
This is my Grandma's recipe

4oz Plain Flour

8 fluid oz milk

2 eggs

Bread

For the toppings   Syrup
                    Lemon
                    Fruit

Why I like Grindleford Primary School
"I grew up here and it's a great place to be."
Elfie Burn (Year 5)

Place flour in bowl and make a well in the middle. Crack the eggs into the well and mix; then add milk and whisk. Heat some oil in a frying pan. Dip slice of bread into mixture and place in pan, frying both sides until golden brown. Remove from pan and add topping of your choice.

THE HARBY HOUSE CHOCOLATE COOKIE TRIFLE

1-1$\frac{1}{2}$ cans of custard
Large bar of white chocolate
Sherry
1 large carton of double cream
2 packets of chocolate chip cookies
Grated milk chocolate

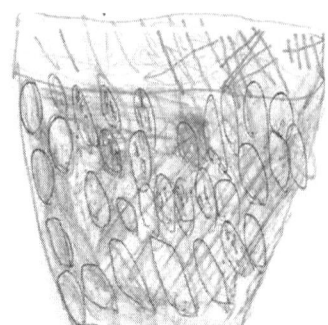

Whip cream and set aside. Melt the chocolate and mix with $\frac{3}{4}$ of the custard. Dip $\frac{1}{2}$ of each cookie into the sherry (otherwise they get too soggy) and line the bowl with cookies. Put some custard mixture into the bowl and add another layer of cookies. Repeat layers, ensuring top layer is a layer of cookies. Mix the remainder of the custard with the cream and top the trifle. Decorate with grated milk chocolate. Place in the fridge for at least 1 hour.

VANILLA FUDGE (by Jessica Nolan)

25g Butter
2 Tablespoons of water
1 Table spoon of Golden Syrup
225g Granulated sugar
4 Tablespoons Evaporated Milk

½ Teaspoon of Vanilla Essence

You will need a small square tin.

Grease the small square tin. Put all the ingredients except the vanilla essence into a large heavy-based saucepan. Using a wooden spoon, stir the ingredients gently over a low heat until all the sugar dissolves. Bring to the boil. Boil very gently for 10 minutes, stirring all the time, until it starts to thicken. Remove from the heat and add the vanilla. Beat with a wooden spoon and then pour quickly into a tin. Cut into squares while warm.

ETON MESS (by Jacob Emery)

1lb strawberries

80ml cranberry juice

450ml double or whipping cream

6 ready-made meringues, crushed

Set aside a few nice small whole strawberries. Remove the green tops from the res and throw them away. Chop the strawberries and place in a mixing bowl with he cranberry juice. Cover the bowl with cling film and put in the fridge until ready to use. When it is time to eat, put the cream in a large mixing bowl and whisk. Stir the cream around and round until it gets thicker and stands in soft peaks. Put the meringues into a plastic bag and roughly crush them using a rolling pin. Using a large spoon, gently fold the strawberries, their juices and crushed meringues into the whipped cream. Spoon the strawberry and cream mixture into a large glass serving dish and decorate with the strawberries you set aside. Serve immediately. Enjoy!

FRUIT AND CHOC FONDUE (By Sam Fletcher)

Mixed Fruit (e.g. strawberries bananas and cherries)
200g Chocolate
150mls Cream
50g butter
1 teaspoon vanilla essence

Cut the fruit into bite sized pieces and put onto cocktail sticks. Next place the chocolate, cream and butter in a bowl over hot water. Stir until melted and mixed. Dunk the fruit into the mixture and enjoy!

Australian Crunchie

200g Margarine (8oz)
125g caster sugar (5oz)
75g desiccated coconut (3oz)
50g cornflakes crushed (2½oz)
1 x 15ml spoon cocoa (1 tbsp)
125g Self raising flour (5oz)

1. Melt Margarine over a low heat
2. Gradually work in the dry ingredients.
3. Press firmly into a greased swiss roll tin
4. Bake in a moderate oven 190°C 375°F Gas mark 5 for 30 mins.
5. Cut into pieces while warm. When cold coat with melted chocolate.

Recipe from the Old Cookbook by Barbara Bater (Barbara's children Alex and Robert were former pupils at Grindleford Primary School)

LEAVERS MEAL 2012

At the end of each school year, the children who are due to leave take part in the Leavers Meal. This magnificent feast is cooked at the school and parents of the leavers are invited to attend. However it is not just a meal. The whole event is managed by the children themselves. Firstly they have to order all the ingredients; and when the day arrives they form groups to prepare and cook the food. As you can see from the menu for 2012 there is no lack of ambition in their choices! It provides a memorable day for the leavers, their families and the school staff.

Our thanks have to go to all the parents, staff and children who contributed to this successful event - both past, present and future

STARTERS

SUMMER CRUNCH SALAD

Serves 4

200g pack small button mushrooms, finely sliced
juice of 1 lemon
200g green beans, trimmed

Handful of soft green herbs, such as basil, chervil, parsley
and tarragon
100g cherry tomatoes, quartered
3 tablespoons olive oil
75g parmesan (or vegetarian alternative), shaved into large
curls

In a bowl, toss mushrooms with half the lemon juice and set
aside - the lemon juice will soften the mushrooms. Blanch the
beans in boiling salted water for 5-6 minutes until they still
have a crunch, but they are not squeaky, then drain and cool
in iced water.

Toss the beans and mushrooms together in a bowl with some
herbs and season with salt and pepper. Toss through the
tomatoes, remaining lemon juice and the olive oil and scatter
with Parmesan just before serving.

ROASTED TOMATO SOUP WITH A PUREE OF BASIL

1½lb (700g) ripe red tomatoes
1 fat clove garlic, chopped
1 small bunch fresh basil leaves
1x4oz (110g) potato
15floz (425ml) boiling water
1 heaped teaspoon tomato puree

1 teaspoon balsamic vinegar
approx. 3 tablespoons extra virgin olive oil
salt and freshly milled black pepper
Solid, shallow roasting tray approx 13x13 inches (33 x33 cm)

First of all skin the tomatoes by pouring boiling water over them, then leave them for 1 minute exactly before draining them and slipping off the skins (protect your hands with a cloth if necessary). Now slice each tomato in half, arrange the halves on the roasting tray, cut side uppermost, and season with salt and pepper. Sprinkle a few drops of olive oil on to each one followed by the chopped garlic, and finally top each one with a piece of basil leaf (dipping the basil into oil first to get a good coating).

Now pop the whole lot into the oven and roast the tomatoes for 50 minutes - 1 hour or until the edges are slightly blackened - what happens in this process is that the liquid in the tomatoes evaporates and concentrates their flavour, as do the roasted edges. About 20 minutes before the end of the roasting time, peel and chop the potato, place it in a saucepan with some salt, 15 fl oz (425ml) of boiling water and the tomato puree and simmer for 20 minutes.

When the tomatoes are ready, remove them from the oven and scrape them with all their juices and crusty bits into a food processor (a spatula is best for this), then add the contents of the potato saucepan and whizz everything to a not-too-uniform puree. If you want to, you can now sieve out the seeds but we left them in to improve the texture.

Just before serving the soup - which should be reheated very gently - make the basil puree by stripping the leaves into a mortar, sprinkling with $\frac{1}{4}$ teaspoon of salt, then bashing the leaves down with a pestle. It takes a minute or two for the leaves to collapse down and become a puree, at which point add 2 tablespoons of olive oil and the balsamic vinegar and stir well.

To serve the soup, pour it into warmed serving bowls and drizzle the basil puree on to the surface, giving a marbled effect.

Tip.   If you make the puree in advance, store it in a cup with clingfilm pressed on to the surface and it will keep its colour - even overnight!

Why I like Grindleford Primary School.......
"Because of the Children!"
Mrs Hill

MAIN COURSE

BEEF WELLINGTON

400g beef fillet
400g flat mushrooms
4 slices Parma ham
English mustard for brushing meat
200g puff pastry
2 egg yolks

1 clove garlic, crushed
1 sprig thyme

Serves 2. Pre-heat oven to 200°C

Heat some oil in a large pan and quickly fry the seasoned beef all over until it's brown. Remove and allow to cool. The point of this is simply to sear the beef and seal all those juices in, you don't want to cook the meat at this stage. Allow to cool and brush generously with the mustard.

Roughly chop the mushrooms and blend in a food processor to form a puree. Scrape the mixture into a hot, dry pan and allow the water to evaporate. When sufficiently dry (the mixture should stick together easily), set aside and cool.

Roll out a generous length of cling film, lay out the four slices of Parma ham, each one slightly overlapping the last. With a pallet knife spread the mushroom texture evenly over the ham.

Place the beef fillet in the middle and keeping a tight hold of the cling film from the outside edge, neatly roll the Parma ham and mushrooms over the beef into a tight barrel shape. Twist the ends to secure the cling film. Refrigerate for 10-15 minutes, this allows the Wellington to set and helps keep the shape.

Roll out the pastry quite thinly to a size which will cover your beef. Unwrap the meat from the cling film. Egg wash the edge of the pastry and place the beef in the middle. Roll up the pastry, cut any excess off the ends and fold neatly to the 'underside'. Turnover and egg wash over the top. Chill again to let the pastry cool, approximately 5 minutes. Egg wash again before baking at 200°C for 35-40 minutes. Rest 8-10 minutes before slicing.

Tip: We cut up our beef into slices and made individual Wellingtons for the Leaver's dinner.

ROAST VEGETABLE TART

Makes 18 Primary age child portions

18oz/500g Puff pastry sheet
8oz/227g Onion, cut into small wedges
8oz/227g Red pepper, cut into large pieces
8oz/227g Carrots, cut into 1 inch chunks
8oz/227g Tomatoes, freshly quartered
5oz/142g Cheese, grated
2 tablespoons/30g Mango chutney
One Beaten egg

Place the prepared vegetables on a greased tin, drizzle with a little oil and roast in a hot oven until golden. Line a roasting tin with the pastry, leaving a 1 inch overlap for the sides. With a sharp knife, score along the overlap edge, but without cutting right through the pastry. The edges will puff up and enclose the filling. Spread the mango chutney thinly over the pastry and top with the roasted vegetables. Sprinkle over the cheese and brush the pastry edges with the beaten egg. Bake in a hot oven until the pastry is risen and golden and the cheese has melted.

You can use a round pastry cutter to make individual tarts if you prefer.

SMALL PORK PIES WITH QUAIL'S EGGS

Makes 6 individual pies

For the hot water crust pastry:
200g/7oz plain flour
40g/1 1/2 oz strong white flour
50g/1 3/4 oz unsalted butter, cut into cubes
100ml/ 3 1/2 fl oz water
 1 teaspoon salt
60g/ 2 1/4 oz lard

For the filling:
6 quail's eggs
1 onion, very finely chopped
350g/12oz pork loin, finely chopped
100g/3 1/2oz unsmoked streaky bacon, finely chopped
small bunch of parsley, finely chopped
sea salt and freshly ground black pepper
1 free-range egg, beaten
1 chicken stock cube
150ml/5fl oz boiling water
2 leaves gelatine

Preheat the oven to 200°C/400F/Gas 6. Grease a 6 hole muffin tin.

To make the pastry, sift the flours into a bowl and rub in the butter until the mixture resembles breadcrumbs. Bring the water and salt to a boil then add the lard and stir until the lard has melted.

Pour the lard and water over the flour mixture and stir in to form a dough. Tip the dough onto a floured work surface and work into a smooth ball (you must work quickly or the dough will become too firm to handle).Roll the pastry out to a thickness of about 3mm. Cut out six 15cm/6in circles and use each to line a hole in the muffin tin. Cut six 10cm/4in circles for the lids and set them aside. For the filling, cook the quail's eggs in a pan of boiling water for two minutes then refresh in cold water, peel carefully and set aside.

Put the onion, pork, bacon and parsley into a bowl, season with salt and freshly ground black pepper and mix well until combined. Spoon a little of the mixture into each pie case, place a quail's egg in the centre and spoon over a little more filling. Brush the edge of each pie case with a little beaten egg, place the lids on top and crimp the edges together to seal completely. Make a small hole in the centre of each pie and bake in the oven for 40 minutes.

When the pies are cooked, set them aside to cool for 10 minutes. Dissolve the stock cube in the boiling water. Soak the gelatine in a little cold water until soft then squeeze out excess water and whisk into the warm chicken stock.

Pour the gelatine mixture into the hole in the top of each pie until the hollow cavity within the pie is filled. Allow the pies to set in the fridge overnight.

Tip.   You can miss out the gelatine bit and serve the pies with a slightly hollow centre. They still taste really nice! (This was the way they were served on Leavers Meal day - due to time constraints!)

TOAD IN THE HOLE

Serves 4

Sunflower oil
8 large, good quality sausages
4 sprigs of fresh rosemary
2 large red onions, peeled and sliced
2 cloves of garlic, peeled and finely sliced
2 knobs of butter
6 tablespoons balsamic vinegar
1 level tablespoon good quality vegetable stock powder or 1 vegetable stock cube

For the batter:
285ml milk
115g plain flour
a pinch of salt
3 eggs

Mix the batter ingredients together and put to one side. To get the batter to go huge, the key thing is to have an appropriately sized baking tin - the thinner the better - as the oil needs to get smoking hot.

Put 1cm/just under 1/2 inch of sunflower oil into a baking tin, then place this on the middle shelf of the oven at its highest setting (240-250°C/475F/gas9). Place a larger tray underneath to catch any oil that overflows from the tin while cooking. When the oil is very hot, add the sausages. Keep your eye on them and allow them to colour until lightly golden.

At this point, take the tin out of the oven, being very careful, and pour the batter mixture over the sausages. Throw a couple of sprigs of rosemary into the batter. It will bubble and possible even spit a little, so carefully put the tin back into the oven, and close the door. Don't open it for at least 20 minutes, as Yorkshire puddings can be a bit temperamental when rising. Remove from the oven when it is golden and crisp.

For the onion gravy, simply fry off your onions and garlic in the butter on a medium heat for about 5 minutes until they go sweet and translucent. You could add a little thyme or rosemary if you like. Add the balsamic vinegar and allow it to cook down by half. At this point, add the stock cube or powder and add a little bit of water. Allow to simmer and you'll have a really tasty onion gravy.

Tip.   We added some red wine to our onion gravy to give our leaver's meal a bit more of a kick!

DESSERTS

SCONES (TO SERVE WITH AFTER DINNER COFFEE)

Makes 8-12 scones

225g/8oz self raising flour
pinch of salt
55g/2oz butter
25g/1oz caster sugar
150ml/5fl oz milk
1 free-range egg, beaten

Heat the oven to 220°C/425F/Gas7. Lightly grease a baking sheet. Mix together the flour and salt and rub in the butter. Stir in the sugar and then the milk to get a soft dough.

Turn out onto a floured work surface and knead very lightly. Pat out to a round area, 2cm/ 3/4inch thick. Use a 5cm/2in cutter to stamp out rounds and place onto the greased baking sheet. Lightly knead together the rest of the dough and stamp out more scones to use it all up.

Brush the tops of the scones with the beaten egg. Bake for 12-15 minutes until well risen and golden.

Cool on a wire rack and serve with butter, good jam and maybe some clotted cream.

Tip.   We wanted to make mini scones as we knew our parents would be quite full up by coffee time, so used a very small cutter instead.

APPLE CRUMBLE

For the basic crumble topping:
8oz/225g plain flour
5oz/150g soft brown sugar
3oz/75g butter, softened at room temperature
1 level teaspoon of baking powder
And:

At least 2lb/900g of Bramley apples, peeled and sliced

Preheat the oven to Gas 4/350F/180°C.

Place the flour in a large mixing bowl, sprinkle in the baking powder, then add the butter and rub it into the flour lightly, using your fingertips. When it all looks crumbly, and the fat has been dispersed fairly evenly, add the sugar and combine that well with the rest of the mixture.

Place the apple slices into a pie dish and sprinkle the crumble mixture all over the fruit. Spread the mixture out evenly using a fork.

Place the crumble on a high shelf in the oven and bake for 30-40 minutes or until the top is tinged with brown.

Tips! Variations on the crumble topping:

Instead of all the flour, use 4oz/110g wholewheat flour and 4oz/110g jumbo or porridge oats. OR...

Instead of all the flour, use 4oz/110g wholewheat flour and 4oz/110g muesli. OR...

For a nut crumble topping, use 6oz/175g wholewheat flour and 3oz/75g chopped nuts. You will need to use only 3oz of soft brown sugar with the 3oz of butter. (We chose to do the oaty topping for our crumble at leaver's meal)

VICTORIA SPONGE

225g/8oz butter or margarine, softened at room
temperature
225g/8oz caster sugar
4 medium eggs
2 teaspoons vanilla extract
225g/8oz self raising flour
milk, to loosen

Preheat the oven to 180°C.

Grease and line two 18cm cake tins with baking paper. Cream
the butter and the sugar together in a bowl until pale and
fluffy. Beat in the eggs, a little at a time, and stir in the
vanilla extract. Fold in the flour using a large metal spoon,
adding a little extra milk if necessary, to create a batter
with a soft dropping consistency. Divide the mixture between
the cake tins and gently spread out with a spatula. Bake in the
oven for 20-25 minutes, or until golden brown on top and
skewer inserted into the middle comes out clean.

Remove from the oven and set aside for 5 minutes, then
remove from the tins and peel off the paper. Place onto a
wire rack.

When cool, sandwich the cakes together with jam, lemon curd or whipped cream and berries.

(We decided to use jam, cream and strawberries for our cake.)

Illustration by Joe Luscombe

THE GRINDLEFORD GALLOP

www.grindlefordgallop.co.uk

The annual Grindleford Gallop is not for the faint hearted. It is both a gruelling fell race for keen runners and a walk for those who take life at a more leisurely pace. The runners will set off together whereas the walkers can choose to start throughout the morning.

Covering approximately 21 miles and 3000ft of ascent, the course takes in the Peak District villages of Grindleford, Froggatt, Eyam, Great Longstone, Edensor and Baslow linking them together with paths, tracks and open moorland of the White Peak. Famous landmarks on the way round include the Riley Graves, Longstone moor, the Monsal Trail and the stunning Chatsworth Park estate. The final high-level section along Baslow, Curbar and Froggatt edges gives breath-taking views of the surrounding Peak District.

On finishing, the weary athletes are treated to cakes and hot drinks which have become part of the Gallop appeal and tradition. The cake recipes were a closely guarded secret - until now! Read on to find the recipes enjoyed by fell race champions and determined walkers alike.

The event is organised by volunteers and all proceeds go to the Grindleford School Parent-Teacher association.

SHARP LEMON SLICES

4 egg
9oz (250g) soft margarine
90z (250 g) caster sugar
12oz (350g) SR flour
2 tsp baking powder
6tbsp milk
Lemon rind 2 lemons
For the Icing
5tblsp lemon juice
120oz(350g) icing sugar

Mix all ingredients in a bowl, beat well
Line a large roasting tin (25 by 10cm) and grease,
Bake @ 180°C or Gas mark 5 for 20-30 mins
Icing ; warm the lemon juice, mix sugar and beat until smooth,
spread on cake and leave to set
Cut into 14/16 slices
Tip: For a crunchy topping use granulated or caster sugar
instead of icing sugar

CHOCOLATE FUDGY SLICES

5 eggs
6tblsp boiling water
9oz(250g) soft margarine
2oz(50g) cocoa
9oz(250g) caster sugar

10oz(274g) self raising flour
3level tsp baking powder
3 tblsp milk
8oz(225g) apricot jam
For the icing:
12oz(350g) icing sugar
2oz(50g) margarine
2oz (50g) cocoa
3tblsp milk

Measure cocoa, mix with boiling water to smooth paste, add
all remaining ingredients except jam
Spread into 25 by 10cm roasting tin, lined and greased. Bake
at 180°C or Gas 5 for 20-30 minutes
For the icing: Melt margarine, add cocoa, add icing and milk
mix until smooth, cool and pour over cake.
Cut when set into slices 14-16.

FRUITY TRAY BAKE

4 eggs
9oz(250g) soft margarine
9oz(250g) caster sugar
12oz(350g) SR flour
4tblsp milk
12oz(350g) mixes dried fruit
A little Demerara sugar

Add all ingredients into bowel except Demerara sugar. Beat well. Grease tin 9 by 14 inches. Add mixture bake @ 180 C for 20-30 minutes. Cool and sprinkle Demerara sugar. Cut into 14-16 slices.

WITH THANKS TO OUR SPONSORS

If you would like to sponsor this book or have any comments please contact
grindleford.cookbook@gmail.com

CALVER SERVICE STATION

The local store with more

Groceries—Newspapers

Hot Food to eat on the go—Salads

Freshly made sandwiches

Coffee's— Flowers

Breads & Milk

Confectionary

Medical supplies

BP Fuel

Air and Vax

Coal, Logs and Charcoal

Beers, Wines & Spirits

Fresh Fruit and Veg

The National Lottery

Nectar points

Pay Point—A.T.M. Machine

E T White & Sons Ltd

Opening Times: Mon—Sat 7am 9pm:
Sunday 8am - 9pm
Telephone 01433-631987

EYAM HALL
BUTTERY

In the grounds of Historic Eyam Hall

Open Daily
10:30am – 4:30pm April to September
Tuesday to Sunday 10:30am – 4:30pm October to March

Morning Coffee, Light Lunches, Afternoon Tea
Homemade Cakes & Scones, Speciality Teas and Coffees
Local Ice Cream

Telephone 01433 630505

194

    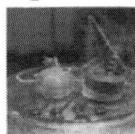

naturalearth
P R O D U C T S

- natural stone tiles
- hand carved fire surrounds
- wooden flooring
- multi-fuel stoves
- fireplace restoration

Suppliers of
CLEARVIEW STOVES
Lining & installation service

01433 631333

info@naturalearthproducts.co.uk
www.naturalearthproducts.co.uk

Showroom at:
Eyam New Road
Grindleford
Hope Valley
Derbyshire
S32 2HW

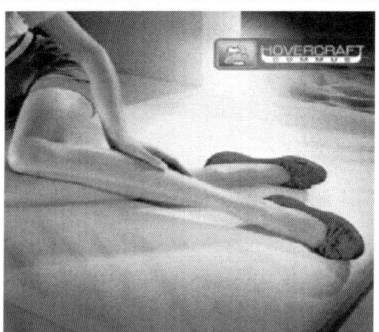

TIDESWELL SCHOOL OF FOOD

WE'RE SERVING UP INSPIRATIONAL COOKERY COURSES FOR ALL ABILITIES TASTES AND BUDGETS.

FROM BAKING BREAD TO THAI COOKING, SAUSAGE MAKING AND BEER BREWING, OUR COURSES ARE CERTAIN TO WHET YOUR APPETITE.

And by booking a course at Tideswell School of Food you are supporting the wider community aims and objectives of the Taste Tideswell project.

For more information or to book a course call us on 01298 871262 or visit our website.

www.tideswellschooloffood.co.uk

Property Renovators

Building on Success

Andrew Carr Farm, Sheffield, South Yorkshire, S35 8QD
Tel 01142 507327   07855 527430

PROPERTY RENOVATORS
SPECIALISTS IN RESIDENTIAL BUILDING

Property Renovators are builders specialising in residential and commercial work in Sheffield and surrounding areas.

WE CAN HELP WITH:

New Build

Extensions

Barn Conversions

Loft conversions

Internal and external alterations

We will handle the whole process of the building works including the initial design, obtaining planning permission and complying with building regulations. For more details on how we work take a look at our process:

Free initial on-site consultation

Full measured survey of your property

Drawings prepared to your specification

Local authority applications

Fully comprehensive survey for a fixed fee

Property Renovators is an experienced and dynamic building company that specialises in designing extensions. Our Surveyors and Architectural Technicians have a wealth of experience across the whole spectrum of residential property types and sizes, and are committed to providing a high quality customer focused service.

We pride ourselves on supplying a customer focused service. For example we have invested in the latest estimating software to enable us to give you a firm quotation, construction program and cash flow chart

For your free initial consultation please contact 01142 507327.

Have you visited the White Lion at Great Longstone?

Open 7 days a week. Booking advisable.

Food service times:
Mon – Fri 12-2.30pm & 6-9pm | Sat 12-9pm | Sun 12-8pm

www.whiteliongreatlongstone.co.uk

The White Lion   Tel: 01629 640 252

Main Street | Great Longstone | Bakewell

ANDREW'S

Door-to-Door Holidays

Day Excursions many local pick-up points

'Team / Party / Corporate' Coach for Hire

Executive & Mini Coaches
for hire from 8 to 75 seats

For FREE brochures call

01298 871222

Anchor Garage, Tideswell, Buxton, Derbyshire
Email   info@andrews-of-tideswell.co.uk
www.andrews-of-tideswell.co.uk

The Barrel Inn, Bretton

Nr. Eyam, Hope Valley S32 5QD

Telephone 01433 630856

The Barrel Inn is the Highest Pub in Derbyshire with views over five counties. Inside, the 16th Century Inn is a delight, with roaring log fires, home cooked food and hand pulled Real Ale. First Class en-suite bedrooms available.

The ideal place for an evening out
A warm and friendly welcome at any time of year

For more information visit our website at **www.thebarrelinn.co.uk**

STEPHEN J BLOWEN

Qualified Domestic Electrician
Based in Grindleford
FOR ALL ELECTRICAL INSTALLATION WORK (Part P)
Also all aspects of plumbing undertaken

Extra lights & sockets, total rewiring to meet current regulations, garden & outside lighting, a burst pipe, new tap washer or a new kitchen/bathroom refit, plastering and tiling to complete the job

Free estimates – Testimonials available

Tel: 01433 639 685 or Mobile: 07818 693 384

Email: stephen_blowen@yahoo.co.uk

Educational Visual Analysis

Phone: 01943 601488

Mobile: 07941 827695

Email: chris@eva-education.co.uk

Web: www.eva-education.co.uk

EVA provides schools with interactive visual reports of their KS2, KS3, GCSE and A-Level teacher assessment grades/levels, mock or examination grades. EVA uses a unique "Dashboard" approach to view all your key performance measures at school, class, form and pupil levels. These dashboards are fully interactive allowing you to filter and highlight the visual data to produce your selected pupil intervention lists in a matter of seconds!

EVA prides itself on offering a "personal" service to our schools. We do not simply provide a "single report that fits all" but we work with schools to ensure our reports are truly embedded into their assessment methodology.

MOUNT PLEASANT
GARAGE

GRINDLEFORD

M.O.T. Testing - Servicing and
Repairs - Welding

Work carried out at competitive rates

Summer @ Calver!

We pride ourselves on the quality of our carefully selected plants.
Now's the time to choose from a wide range of stunning flowers to add a flourish and splendour to your garden.

**Calver Sough Nurseries,
Hassop Road,
Calver.
S32 3XH.
Tel: 01433 630692**
http://www.calversoughgardencentre.com

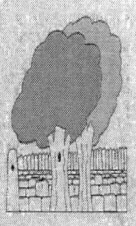

Girlguiding UK
girls in the lead

1st Curbar Guides meet on Monday evenings in term time from 7:00pm till 8:30pm.

Our activities include: camping, crafts, outdoor cooking, trips out and challanges.
Guides is a great way to make new friends and learn new skills.

For more information, please contact Carolyn on 01433630560

SMILE

Stoney Middleton Interest & Leisure Enterprise have improved facilities on the playing field in the village and have maintained the equipment for 16 years. Visit:

www.stoneymiddletonsmile.yolasite.com

to follow our progress and to find out how you might be able to support our work

INDEX

T

V

W